in OUR HOOD

This copy is signed

Book and cover design by Jacob Covey.
Book printing by Alphagraphics, Seattle.

ISBN 0-9779832-3-4
826 Seattle
8414 Greenwood Avenue North
P.O. Box 30764
Seattle, Washington 98113
(206) 725-2625
www.826seattle.org

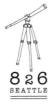

826 SEATTLE

52 short plays you can perform in any place

by Students of Hamilton International Middle School and 826 Seattle Students

Foreword by Ramón Esquivel

FOREWORD

Playwriting will save the universe.

Should our civilization embrace this maxim, educators around the world will teach the craft of playwriting in schools. Learning the elements of dramatic narrative -- character, conflict, and action -- will be as fundamental to a child's education as learning the alphabet, articulating democratic principles, memorizing multiplication tables, and explaining the process of natural selection. Pre-schoolers still learning how to read will dictate tiny dramas about territorial conflicts in sandboxes. Elementary school students will pen puppet plays about fairness and justice on the soccer field. Middle school students will script fantastical allegories about the epic struggle between good and evil. High school students will dramatize that struggle in shades of gray in hallways at school. The rite of passage will be writing a one-hour play instead of taking a four-hour standardized test. Each successive generation of human beings will understand each other better. Nations will be at peace. The universe will be saved.

Not convinced? Sensible skepticism is healthy. Allow me to elaborate.

Consider what a playwright needs. Characters and dialogue drive the action of a play. A playwright must study and (try to) understand human beings and the ways we communicate with each other and navigate the world. A playwright is the mind of each character in the drama, mentally shifting from one point-of-view to another. She imagines their deepest desires, their most transcendent joys, and their darkest fears. She finds their motivations for action. She anticipates their responses to adversity. To do all this, a playwright must empathize with every character she creates, from her most heroic protagonist to her most loathsome antagonist. Above all, a playwright needs empathy.

        To nurture empathy, a playwright listens with his ears and eyes and emotional antennae. "Put yourself in someone else's shoes" is not just a saying but a strategy for understanding characters. Imagine a child who has learned that spoken words have power, that people communicate with more than their voices, that we all share a rather small set of basic desires -- survival, self-determination/freedom, and connection, to name a few -- and that these basic desires motivate all human behavior. Now imagine that same child intuits that his own voice has power, that he can convey the range of human emotion through his body language, that his desires are basically the same as everyone else's, and that pursuing those desires requires action. Playwriting is conducting a lab experiment to test theories of living.

        826 Seattle recognizes this.

        Each student that is published in this book learned why the word playwright is spelled the way it is. A play is not something that is written; a play is something that is wrought. These playwrights engaged each other in enthusiastic brainstorming sessions, made tough decisions, had joyous epiphanies, survived awkward read-throughs, perhaps envied the ideas and skills of their peers, and persevered. Through it all, there was always a shared sense of tribulation and triumph. These playwrights grew as a community of artisans.

        In Our Hood celebrates their hard work more as a portfolio of artwork than as an anthology of writing. Plays, like paintings or dances, are meant to be seen and experienced. To truly appreciate the playwrights' craft, gather some friends and perform their scripts in your home, in your classroom, on a playground, or in your imaginations. Then, invent characters of your own. What do they want? How will they get it? Listen to how your friends speak to each other. Create a story inspired by people you know. Understand that you can learn playwriting, too, if are willing to work hard.

        The universe needs you.

                                        - Ramón Esquivel
                                          Playwright & Teacher

Table of of
Contents

Ch. 3: RELATIONSHIPS

Ch. 4: DRAMA

Ch. 5: SPORTS

Ch. 6: INDIE

Chapter 1

Action/ Adventure

Estefany Sahagun
Tara Phenix-Touslee

"AN HOUR TIL DOOM"

(PACO, ALLISON and ADRIAN are at the ski resort.)

NARRATOR   Everything started on bright shiny Saturday
with Paco, Adrian, and Allison. The three 14-year-olds had been
best friends since the third grade. Throughout that time, Paco
and Adrian had had a crush on Allison but neither had ever had
the guts to say it. Not until that one Saturday they wanted to
snowboard, just the three friends.

SNOW LIFT GUY   Ready? Ready? Sit down and keep your snowboards
up.

PACO   We know, we know, it's not the first time we've
done this.

ALLISON   Paco, you don't have to be so rude.

ADRIAN   Ha ha! She likes me better.

NARRATOR   The snow lift went up and up.

PACO   No, she does not, and do you know why?

ADRIAN   No, why? The only girl that likes you is
your mom!

PACO   Okay, you went too far! Keep my mom out
of this!

NARRATOR   The snowlift rocked back and forth as Paco
accidentally pushed Allison off. They all went tumbling down,
holding onto each other.

ALLISON   Help!

PACO   Hold onto my board, Allison!

ADRIAN   Paco, hold onto my board, and don't let go!

NARRATOR   Allison was holding onto Paco and Paco was
holding onto Adrian, who was holding onto the snow lift.

SNOW LIFT GUY   (singing to himself)

                 Bam bam bam bbam bam bam bam bbam bam bam... I
used to rule the world! I love Viva La Vida...

        (He notices that the three friends are falling off the
lift.)

                 Oh my god!

        (He starts speaking into a walkie-talkie.)

                 This is 417 Roger! There appears to be three
kids hanging off a chair lift! We need back up!

        (A VOICE comes through the walkie-talkie.)

VOICE   Roger, this is 317! We're bringing up a big
inflatable trampoline and rescue officers! Stop the chair lift!

SNOW LIFT GUY   Roger that!

ALLISON   I'm scared, you guys! Please don't let go, you
morons.

PACO   Don't be scared! I'm right here, and I won't
let you go, don't worry.

ADRIAN   Hey, hello, I'm the one that's carrying the two
of you. I don't at least get a thanks? How rude.

PACO   Hey, you guys! The chair lift stopped! I think they saw us! We're saved!

ADRIAN   Oh, yeah? Isn't hay for horses, not for people?

PACO   You said the same thing, so shut up. Hey, you
guys! I think I see a helicopter and an ambulance. I love you
Alison! And I also see a trampoline.

ALLISON   What did you say?

PACO   I saw a helicopter.

ALLISON   After that.

PACO   I saw an ambulance.

ALLISON   After that.

PACO   A trampoline.

ALLISON   Spit it out.

PACO   Okay, okay, I still like you. I have liked you
since the third grade.

ADRIAN   Me too. I love you! Ha, I loved you first.

ALLISON   You guys, I'm not ready for this. Let's just be
friends, okay? This is not the right time to be talking about
this. Also, our lives are in danger. Hello!

ADRIAN   But...

ALLISON   Promise!

PACO   I promise, Allison.

Anthony Quinto-Tila
Andy Cao

"ISLAND TROUBLES"

(<u>ANDY</u>, <u>ANTWON</u> and <u>BILL</u> are in a boat with a <u>CAPTAIN</u> and other <u>PASSENGERS</u>.)

<u>ANDY</u>   La la la la, wait till I get my money back.

(<u>ANDY</u> sees the island.)

Is that it?

(They are wet from the huge waves.)

<u>ANTWON</u>   Yeah! Bill, look!

<u>BILL</u>   Where am I? I thought we were going to the new McDonald's?

(The sand shimmers and you can see the trees.)

<u>ANTWON</u>   On the Galapagos Islands? No way! Why would there be a McDonald's here?

(He gets out of the boat.)

<u>BILL</u>   It's a weird island. I want some mangos.

(He walks toward a forest.)

<u>ANDY</u>   Nice going, Antwon. You doo-doo head.

<u>ANTWON</u>   It's not my fault!

(<u>ANDY</u> and <u>ANTWON</u> look like they are about to fight.)

BILL   You both be quiet!

ANDY & ANTWON   What? Why?

BILL   Dang, calm down. Dude, we are so lost.

ANDY   What, we are?! Jeez, you are so messed up!

BILL   Dude, why are we even here?

ANDY   Because of Antwon and that dumb tree!

BILL   Why you gotta say that?

ANDY   Me?! Tch wow.

ANTWON   What th...

BILL   Man, we aren't even friends!

ANDY   Uhhh... We are.

BILL   Oh, yeah? Hah.

ANDY   Ugh.

BILL   Man! Stop acting like you're the man of
the house!

ANDY   Me?

        (BILL and ANDY start to fight.)

ANTWON   Dude!

        (ANTWON slaps BILL and ANDY.)

ANTWON   C'mon guys, let's just go back to the boat.

BILL & ANDY   Fine!

        (They stomp out of the forest.)

BILL   I still want to go to McDonald's.

ANDY & ANTWON   Shut up.

ANTWON   First... wait!

ANDY & BILL   What?

ANTWON   We need to work together to go back to the boat. But first, we need food. So, Andy, you get the wood for warmth, and Bill you get fish, and I will find some fruit.

ANDY & BILL   Alright.

(One hour later, as they went back to the boat, all of the fifteen passengers were on the surface. But then... SWOOSH! The boat sank, going down slowly into the water. Bloop, Bloop, Bloooop.)

PASSENGER 1   Oh my...

PASSENGER 2   Oh for...

PASSENGER 3   Oh no!

CAPTAIN   My boat! My beautiful cruise!

(Awkward silence.)

ANTWON   I brought mangos.

(Everybody looks at ANTWON like he was some drunken guy who didn't see anything. Suddenly, ANTWON saw the boat blooping.)

ANTWON   Ahhhhhhhhhhhhhh! We're Stuck! Ahhhhhh!

(ANTWON runs in circles. Now the passengers really think he's drunk. Bushes sway, it feels a bit cold.)

PASSENGER 1   Something is in there!

ANTWON   CHUPACABRA! Ahhhhhh!

PASSENGERS,
BILL & ANDY   Shut Up!

ANDY   It is just a little boy!

LITTLE BOY   Oh… Hello? What are you doing here? You guys
are on the coast side of the island.

ANTWON   Aha, what now? Is this Galapagos?

        (As they follow the boy, they see forest animals, look
at the very old turtles and are having fun.)

ALL   We are here! Finally!

RANGER   Sorry for what happened! We'll ask a different
captain to pick you guys up. Feel free to look around.

CAPTAIN   B-but, my boat!

ANTWON,
ANDY & BILL   Oh well, at least we are still here, and not
still in that boat.

BILL   I still want to go to McDoanld's!

ANTWON & ANDY   Shut up!

BILL   Say please!

ANTWON & ANDY   No thanks.

Evan Adams
Jonathan Tran

"THE STALKER OF HALLOWEEN"

(EVAN comes to the front door of CHET's house.)

EVAN   Hey Chet! How's it going?

CHET   Good, how's your day?

EVAN   Okay.

CHET   Hey, how many pieces of candy do you think we will collect for Halloween?

EVAN   100,000 pieces of candy!

CHET   Come on, you really think we're going to collect that much candy?

EVAN   Yeah!

CHET   Oh! Come in.

EVAN   Thanks, I thought you'd never ask.

CHET   Ha ha ha! You're funny.

(They enter the house.)

EVAN   Hi, Mr. and Mrs. Merklin. So, Chet lets go play games on the computer!

CHET   Okay.

(They run up the stairs to the computer.)

CHET   Hold up, let me log on!

EVAN   What game are we going to play online?

CHET   We're going to play Final Ninja on Miniclip!

EVAN   Man, your computer is slow!

CHET   I know, I'm supposed to get a new one soon.

EVAN   Finally, let's play! You go first, and when you die. I get to play!

CHET   Okay!

   (A few moments later...)

EVAN   Ha, you died! My turn.

CHET   Okay, go.

   (12 minutes later...)

EVAN   I won and stayed on the longest!

   (Chet's parents call them down for dinner.)

CHET   Okay, we're on our way! One sec, I have to log off and shut down.

EVAN   Okay, I'll meet you down there.

   (They go downstairs.)

EVAN   Wow, Mrs. Merklin, this dinner is awesome!

CHET   Hey, let's go get our costumes on. You first!

EVAN   Okay!

   (EVAN changes into his costume.)

CHET   Nice Batman costume! It looks so real, I mean, with the belt and everything!

EVAN   Thanks! Now get yours.

CHET   Okay!

EVAN   Man, I think you have the best costume out of the whole group. You look like a real zombie. Even the blood looks real.

CHET   Thank you!

EVAN   Come on, Mr. and Mrs. Merklin! Let's go trick or treating.

CHET   Yeah, let's go!

        (They were now at the 30th house of the night.)

EVAN   Hey Chet! Let's separate from the group this year, and go trick or treating by ourselves.

CHET   I don't think that's a good idea.

EVAN   Come on! This is the 30th house in an hour! We'll get more candy if we leave the group.

CHET   But still, we could get lost and...

EVAN   Why, are you scared?

CHET   No! Okay, let's go.

EVAN   Let's sneak away very quietly. Okay, now, run!

CHET   Hey, this is fun.

        (They trick or treated at 12 houses, but on the way to the 13th house a MAN rustles in the bushes.)

EVAN   What was that?

CHET   I don't know, but I think it was a squirrel.

     (They walked slowly and cautiously. The MAN rustles again.)

EVAN   What?

CHET   Uh, what?

EVAN   You said something.

CHET   No, I didn't.

     (MAN slowly creeps out of the bushes, unaware that EVAN has seen him.)

EVAN   We're not alone! There's a guy in a Scream costume behind us!

     (CHET turns around.)

CHET   Huh?

     (The MAN runs towards them. EVAN and CHET scream and run in different directions.)

EVAN   No! Come over here, there's a dead end over there!

CHET   It's all the same!

EVAN   No! This way goes towards home!

CHET   Okay!

     (CHET turns around.)

MAN   Come here!

     (CHET kicks the MAN in the leg, and the MAN falls over.)

EVAN   Come on, let's go!

         (Minutes later...)

CHET   I think we lost him.

EVAN   Come on, we've got to call the police!

         (They run to the nearest phone booth.)

EVAN   Dang it! It doesn't work. Come on, let's go
home.

CHET   Yeah.

         (They hear the MAN rustling in the bushes again.)

CHET   Oh snaps! There he is!

MAN   Come here!

         (EVAN trips. He begins cursing.)

CHET   Look, rocks!

EVAN   So?

CHET   Ehhem?

EVAN   Right! So we throw rocks at him!

         (Two minutes later...)

MAN   Where are you?

CHET   Over here!

MAN   Huh?

EVAN   Throw them!

         (EVAN and CHET throw rocks at him and he runs off.)

CHET   Is he gone?

          (CHET looks around.)

EVAN   Yeah. Let's get out of here.

          (They arrive at home.)

CHET   I can't believe we made it home!

EVAN   Yeah!

Skiah Garde Garcia
Wyatt Lease

"THE ADVENTURES OF CHUCK AND MATI"

(CHUCK is in a tree, talking to MATI.)

CHUCK   Hello, my name is Chuck, and just let me tell
you this: I do not like the city. This is what's happened so
far. I was sitting at my crib, on my branch, when I decided to
go out and have an adventure. Yes I am a squirrel.

(CHUCK shows himself.)

CHUCK   A squirrel with simple needs: Food, water and
some shade. Oh yeah, did I mention that I love sleeping? My
idea of an adventure was to go outside of this park (which is
basically my house), and to go walk around the town. I live in
Madison Park, but now I might have to live in the city. Anyway,
I was walking when a woman kicked me onto a Metro bus by
accident, and the bus drove me to downtown Seattle. I got off
and, well, this is where I am now. Lost in an overpopulated,
gi-normous, loud city.

(He points his arms up.)

MATI   We should fly!

(She lifts her arms to her side and lifts one foot.)

CHUCK   I don't think I can fly. I think we should go
through the sewers, I have a couple of homies down there.

MATI   Mmm, no, let's just say that I don't get along
with alligators. It's not me, it's just pigeons, they don't
like pigeons.

CHUCK   I'm sure they will like you, the alligators at
Madison sewers love chickadees, and you know how annoying those
are!

MATI   Well...

CHUCK   How about first I try to "fly," and then, if
that fails, we go my way?

MATI   Okey-dokey-panokey!

          (MATI flies to the top of a building, as CHUCK is climb-
ing the building. When they get to the top, they look around.)

CHUCK   So, what do I have to do?

MATI   Flap your wings and run off the building. You
will see, ducky.

CHUCK   First of all, I don't have wings. Second of
all, I'm not a ducky!

MATI   I thought I didn't have wings either, but now I
know I do! Soon enough, you will know too.

CHUCK   If I die, it's your fault.

          (CHUCK spreads his arms out, and jumps off the
building, flapping his arms. He falls into some sheets which
were hanging on clotheslines. The sheets wrap around his wrists
creating a parachute, and he lands into an open garbage can.
He pops his head out of the garbage can with a banana peel on
his head, and when MATI flies down, he looks at her, takes the
banana peel off his head, and holds the peel in front of him,
before dropping it.)

CHUCK   Not cool.

          (CHUCK climbs out of the trash can.)

CHUCK   Now let's try my idea.

(CHUCK starts walking.)

CHUCK   The alligators practically own the sewers, and they know the sewers like the back of their tails! They can show us the way out.

          (They stop at a big sewer drain. He opens it and lets MATI go first. Once they are down in the sewer drain, they start walking.)

MATI   It stinks like a garbage can on a summer day.

NARRATOR   And you don't want to smell that!

CHUCK   My friends should be here soon!

NARRATOR   While Chuck was walking, Mati thought she saw and heard an alligator in the water next to her, but she figured she was wrong. But she was right, there was an alligator there. The thing she didn't know was that it was hunting her.

          (The alligator jumps up, out of the water, and almost captures MATI in his mouth. But she flies up to the top of the sewer.)

MATI   Let's get out of here!

CHUCK   Okay, sounds good.

          (They run to the nearest sewer drain and get out, then run out of the street into an alley.)

MATI   Let's not do that again, for shizle!

CHUCK   I know for realzies!

MATI   Well, how are we going to get you home?!

CHUCK   I can run on the telephone wires.

MATI   I could fly, and then tell you which direction to run. So really, I'll be the scout.

NARRATOR   It was set. The next day they were going to look for Madison Park.

        (Birds are chirping and the sun is rising, CHUCK and MATI awaken and head to the nearest power line to get started.)

NARRATOR   After Chuck reminded Mati for the fifth time about what the plan was and what the park looked like, they were off. About three hours later Mati thought she saw Madison Park.

MATI   I see it, I see it!

CHUCK   Lead me to it.

        (About twenty minutes later...)

CHUCK   Ye, yes! This is it!

MATI   YAHOO! We made it!

NARRATOR   It was true that they had made it! They made it!

        (They climb up into CHUCK's tree. Then they sit on the branches together, trying not to get close.)

CHUCK   Well, thank you so much for helping me get back home.

MATI   Yeah! You're welcome, ducky.

CHUCK   Since you don't have a crib, you could live with me. Until we build you a crib of your own, someday. You are now officially my homie!

Kevin Dang
Jonathan Del Cid

"HOBO"

(JAMES is dressed like a hobo when MONICA walks by.)

JAMES   Monica? Can I borrow some money?

MONICA   What happened to you?

JAMES   Man! The mafia is after me.

MONICA   Here's $150, now go and get a job.

(JAMES runs off with the money.)

(Three days later...)

MONICA   Time to watch some TV.

(MONICA turns on the TV.)

MONICA   OH MY GOD!! That (beep), he's gambling all the money I gave him. I'm gonna go and beat him!.

(MONICA drives to The World Series of Poker.)

JAMES   Ah crap, she's here.

MONICA   What are you doing here?

JAMES   I gambled all my money away. Then I borrowed $100 from a guy in the Mafia. Then I got beat up because I didn't pay them back.

MONICA   Here's another hundred bucks. If I catch you here again, I will cut your throat off.

          (MONICA leaves abruptly.)

          (Two weeks later...)

          (There is gunfire. A scream is heard offstage. JAMES kicks open Monica's front door.)

MONICA   What the--!

JAMES   Let me stay here! The Mafia is trying to shoot me down.

MONICA   No!

          (JAMES makes a puppy dog face.)

JAMES   Please?!

MONICA   Fine!

          (Five hours later...)

          (The Mafia comes in and shoots warning shots at the ceiling.)

MONICA   (screams) What the--! You (beep)!

          (She runs, but the Mafia thinks she's going to get away and call the cops, so they shoot at her.)

JAMES   Monica, move! You're going to get shot!

          (JAMES tries to run to her, but he can't. He runs while the Mafia chases him down. MONICA gets shot.)

MONICA   Ahh!

          (JAMES tries to help her but he sees the Mafia coming after him, so he runs for the exit. He sees a motorcycle gang and kicks a guy off his motorcycle.)

JAMES   You can't touch this. So long suckers!

          (The Mafia kicks the rest of the motorcycle gang off
their bikes, and they chase after him. He takes his motorcycle
on a ramp and over a fence into the airport. JAMES falls and
gets cut up, but he gets off and hides under a plane.)

NARRATOR   James broke his leg, and more importantly,
he broke his heart, because of the loss of one of his best
friends.

JAMES   I was so stupid, I gambled all my money away,
and now one of my friends is dead.

NARRATOR   James got a job as a cashier at McDonald's, and
then he became a McDonald's manager and began to pay all his
debts. Then he made his own shoe company called Filthy (beep)
Shoes. He becomes a millionaire in less than five years. Every
day, still, he visits Monica's grave.

          (JAMES puts flowers at her grave, looks up in the sky,
and it starts raining.)

JAMES   MONICA!!!!!

David Gonzalez

"MAGIC MOUNTAIN WAVES"

(RICH BOY, REN and BOB are at Magic Mountain Waves. There is a new ride called Roller-Coaster Splash. Lots of people are there. The boys are dropped off by REN's parents.)

BOB   See you later, Ren's parents. (to friends) Let's go to Roller-Coaster Splash.

RICH BOY   Sure, let's go. I have really been waiting to go on that ride!

REN   I don't really care.

(RICH BOY and BOB run towards Roller-Coaster Splash. But REN just walks behind. They finally get to the ride's line.)

BOB   Rich Boy and Ren, look! There are only two seats left on the ride, and we're next! How are we going to decide which two will go?

RICH BOY   Ren, can you wait for the next group of people?

REN   (shouting) No, Rich Boy! Why don't you?!

RICH BOY   (ordering) No, because Bob and I have been waiting a long time to go on this ride. Four months of waiting! And you don't even care about the ride! So you wait right here and wait for the next group of people.

REN   No! I will not be ordered around by a kid that is younger than me.

RICH BOY   (threatening) If you don't wait right here until the next group of people, I will tell your parents that you're not being cooperative, and you will be in big trouble.

REN   I will not wait, or else I will tell your parents that you are bossing me around.

RICH BOY   But my parents are not in town. I am staying at Bob's house. So you're the one that's going to get into big trouble.

CROWD   (screaming) Get on the ride! We're waiting for you to get on!

REN   I'm getting really frustrated, and I am not in a really good mood. If my parents find out I've been bad, they will take away my video games. And I'm not having that.

BOB   (to the crowd) Just be quiet, already!

MAN IN LINE   Hurry up, because everyone on the ride is waiting for you to get on. If you guys don't hurry up, then the ride will get shut down for the day!

RICH BOY   Okay, so let's just decide. I don't want to miss this ride, and we've already paid for it.

BOB   If you guys don't come up with a solution, we're just all going to have to wait until there are enough seats for all of us. Or else, we won't get on the ride.

REN   Well, okay. I'm going to stay out until the next group of people. So all of us will be able to go.

RICH BOY   You know what? Let's just let the people behind us go, and then we can all three go on the ride at the same time.

REN   You know, that is a great idea.

BOB   But we will have to ask the third person behind us if we can get in front of him.

          (They ask the third person behind them. The stranger is very polite and lets them return to the line in front of him.)

BOB, REN & RICH BOY   Thank you very much, sir!

(The boys are now in the second group, and there are enough chairs for all of them. They get the greatest seats on the ride - they get the front seats!)

BOB   Finally, we came up with a solution and now we're all happy!

(The boys are now on the ride and start screaming in happiness.)

REN   Sorry, Rich Boy and Bob, for screaming at you about the ride, even though it was for nothing. I really didn't care about the ride. At first, I didn't want to go. But now I am thrilled about the ride. I wish I could go again.

BOB   It's okay. I accept your apology.

RICH BOY   It's too bad your parents didn't give you enough money for a second ride and lunch. But good thing I brought extra money! So now we can all go a second time.

REN   I guess that's why they call you Rich Boy. You always have extra money.

(The boys laugh a lot and go back on the ride line for a second time.)

Ryan Dzulkarnaen
Angel Sandoval

"BREAKOUT"

(DUSTIN and MONO are talking in school.)

DUSTIN   Hey, Mono! So you wanna go to the Northgate Mall?

MONO   Sure. When are we going?

DUSTIN   I'll meet you at the bus stop near my house
after school.

(Later, at DUSTIN's house.)

MONO   Hey Rosa!

ROSA   Oh, hey, Mono. You want something?

MONO   No, I'm fine. Where's Dustin?

ROSA   He's in his room.

(MONO goes up to DUSTIN's room.)

MONO   Dude, are you going or not? If you are, then
hurry up. I don't wanna miss the 16.

DUSTIN   Yeah. Let me get my tokens. You want one?

MONO   Yeah, let's go!

DUSTIN   Okay, okay. But I gotta get my wallet first.
It's in the living room, with my keys.

(They go to the living room.)

ROSA   Where are you guys going?

DUSTIN   To the Northgate Mall. We're gonna hang out and possibly get caught by the security.

ROSA   Oh, can I come? I wanna get some new shoes, and a charger for my DS.

DUSTIN   Sure, but hurry up.

        (They arrive at the mall.)

NEARBY TV   There have been reports that Umbrella's new product contains the t-virus, which might cause destruction in this city just like what happened in Raccoon City. The t-virus is a deadly virus that will turn people into zombies! The t-virus has broken out!

POLICEMAN   Everybody out of the building now!

        (The POLICEMAN gets bitten by a zombie, and screams. A siren starts. Zombies start chasing them.)

DUSTIN   Dude, let's go! The zombies are right there! Run!

MONO   (panting) Let's go to GI Joe's! I think they have guns there!

        (They run to GI Joe's.)

DUSTIN   Oh wow. There's only BB guns and metal bullets! Wait, where's Rosa?

        (ROSA is wandering around in the parking lot, wondering where the guys are. She's terrified, and begins to cry.)

ROSA   Dustin, Mono, where are you guys? Why aren't you here?

        (DUSTIN arrives at the parking lot and finds ROSA.)

DUSTIN   There you are, Rosa. Why are you here? I can't believe you! Hurry up, let's go to GI Joe's with Mono before the zombies come!

(DUSTIN and ROSA run to GI Joe's.)

MONO   Let's go! They're coming up the stairs! They're on the third floor! Get inside! Dustin, throw me that clear sub-machine gun and a pack of bullets!

DUSTIN   Okay, I'll help you! Rosa, stay right there! Don't move, and keep a pistol with you just in case, okay!?

ROSA   Okay!

MONO   They're here! Come on, Dustin. Let's do this! Let's save ourselves. Those zombies are going down!

(They shoot the zombies. the zombies fall off the walkway, and the metal bullets ricochet off their heads, pelting everywhere. DUSTIN goes to protect ROSA. The S.W.A.T. arrives and kills the zombies. MONO is caught in the crossfire. ROSA and DUSTIN follow the S.W.A.T. and go to a camp for survivors.)

ROSA   I am going to miss Mono. He was such a good friend. I can't believe he died in that crossfire. We tried so hard.

Chapter 2

Sci-Fi/ Fantasy

Justin Cauble
Sora Ishiwata

"KITCHEN SINK"

OMOSHIROII   Holy crap!!! Aliens are in my neighborhood!
I hope they don't steal my first edition Bionicles!

    (OMOSHIROII gasps as aliens enter.)

STUIE   We have arrived, earthlings! Bring me a Diet
Coke on the rocks!

BROCK   Yes, we have arrived! I'll have a Coke as well.

OMOSHIROII   (in awe) Wow! How did you guys get here?

STUIE   Our spaceship, stupid! Now how about my
Diet Coke?

OMOSHIROII   Sorry! I apologize! We only have Natchan.
So, why are you guys here?

BROCK   Because we came to steal your kitchen sink!

OMOSHIROII   Why just the kitchen sink?

STUIE   Not really the kitchen sink, stupid!

OMOSHIROII   Oh sorry. I did not realize that you wanted the
whole planet.

STUIE   That...

BROCK   Sorry for interrupting, but Steve Madden's
Tonight Show is on in 20 minutes, so we need to get going.

STUIE   Fine! We'll leave this Earthling alone and postpone our kitchen sink taking.

          (The aliens fly away offstage.)

Trinh Nguyen

"CATCHER EQUALS FRIEND"

(MANTA and YOH are hanging out.)

NARRATOR   Once, in a parallel world, there were two kids
who could see ghosts but until one important day, they hadn't
noticed their special ability. The two kids were named Yoh
and Manta. Yoh was a tall, lazy guy, but he never would get
frightened by anyone. He liked to listen to his radio all day.
Manta was a short, smart guy who was scared of anything that
looked scary. Many of his classmates made fun of him because he
was so short. Yoh and Manta were best friends who lived in the
same house and who lived alone with no adult or guardian. They
were both fourteen and they used to go to the graveyard late
at night. They didn't know why they felt compelled to go the
graveyard, but they would anyway.

MANTA   Okay, do you want to watch a movie at my
friend's house? Or we can go to the theater and watch a scary
movie there!

YOH   Okay, but this movie better be good, or you're
wasting time I could be listening to my radio.

NARRATOR   They went to the movie theater and waited for a
long time. When they finally got into the theater...

MANTA   Well, don't worry! I think this movie will
be fascinating.

NARRATOR   Yoh didn't answer, but he looked up and saw
something gray.

YOH   Hey, I see something on the ceiling! It looked
like a human, and it was kind of see-through and it is going
through the ceiling! Ahhh!

AMEDAMARY   Whoa, did he see me? Or did he just see
something else that frightened him?

PEOPLE AROUND YOH Shut up and be quiet! Let me hear the movie! You're hurting my ears!

NARRATOR   Yoh ran out of the theater, running as hard and as far as he could, but then he heard Manta yelling.

MANTA   Hey, wait up! I can't catch up to you! You're going too fast!

NARRATOR   Yoh slowed down and waited for Manta to come, but then he heard a scream and he ran back towards Manta.

YOH   Hey, Manta? Are you there?

NARRATOR   There was a silence. Then Yoh saw Manta lying in the middle of the street.

YOH   Wake up Manta! What are you doing in the middle of the street?

MANTA   Oh, it is nothing, I just got scared of the ghost who was in front of me when I stopped to take a deep breath.

YOH   Hey, you see the ghost too? I wonder if anybody else saw the ghost and ran off. Oh, tell me, what kind of shape is the ghost? Is it a boy or a girl?

MANTA   Whoa, wait up! I have to take a deep breath! The ghost is a boy, and he is naked, wearing only had a hat, so I fainted. I think that the ghost is lonely! His face looked like he was scared, maybe of another ghost or something. But I think that he is looking for someone to play with or someone who can care for him.

        (They hear a mysterious scream.)

YOH   Well, are we going to catch the ghost and become his friend, and stop him from scaring people?

MANTA   Well, let's go then!

NARRATOR   Then, they heard the sound of the cop's loud bell that meant it was time for everyone go to their own house.

MANTA   Yoh, I think we have to go a little bit faster, and we have to stay out of the cop's way, but we have to follow

the sound of the person who just yelled. Hey, Yoh, stop!
I think that the ghost just passed us!

YOH   Okay, we know that the ghost is a boy and that
he is trying to make friends and that he also want someone to
take care of him. He came out of the ceiling and looked at
people, so maybe we should go to the theater and look upstairs!
We might find him there.

NARRATOR   So the next night, they went upstairs and
looked around, and saw that the ghost was sitting in the corner
making a sore face.

YOH   Hey, what are you doing up here all alone and
making that sore face? If you will come with us, we will take
care of you and you don't have to live in the upstairs of this
theater. You can live with us, and nobody will be afraid of you.

AMEDAMARY   No way, I don't want to live with you! You
think that I am so dumb that I would come to your house? What
do you want to do with me, huh?

MANTA   No, I mean, do you want to live with us,
because we don't have anybody else to live with, and you then
can go to school with us. I will get you dressed somehow!

AMEDAMARY   Okay, but how I am going to get dressed, and
keep myself from being naked?

MANTA   I need to know how you have that ghost hat
right there on your head.

AMEDAMARY   Oh this? I got this before I died. It got
buried with me, but my clothes weren't there so now I only have
a hat. Oh yeah, I forgot to tell you, my name is Amedamary and
I am a boy who worked at the theater.

MANTA   Oh, I am Manta and he is Yoh. Okay, I think I
have an idea about how the cop will not find you.

YOH   Okay, but if he gets caught, I am not going to
do anything.

MANTA   Okay, let's see now. That street is dark and
nobody can see us, so the street is not a dangerous place to
go. Okay, let's get going!

YOH   Are you sure this is the right street? I have never been here before, and my legs are getting tired.

MANTA   Yes, I am sure, and we are almost home, but I see someone over there. I see people with some kind of material on their backs.

YOH   Oh, it's probably some people trying to catch the ghost. I think they are because it said so on their van!

MANTA   Then we'd better stay here until they're gone.

YOH   I need to go to the bathroom, but there are so many people here. I don't think I am going to make it.

NARRATOR   Yoh ran to his house and went straight to the bathroom. When he came out, the people introduced themselves to Yoh.

GHOST HUNTER   We are ghost hunters, and we think that you have a ghost in your house. Let us in!

YOH   Oh, what ghost are you talking about?

NARRATOR   The ghost hunters got so confused, but they knew that Yoh was telling a lie.

GHOST HUNTER   Oh yeah? You're not going to trick me!

YOH   Then you should go in and take a look for yourselves.

NARRATOR   They went in, and they didn't find any ghost so they left. Yoh told Manta how he fooled the ghost hunter. Then, all three of the kids came in and locked the door.

MANTA   Where are you going, Amedamary?

AMEDAMARY   I don't know, but I will visit you soon.

NARRATOR   So from that day, Yoh and Manta have waited and waited for Amedamary to come back and visit them, but Amedamary has been nowhere to be seen.

Sophia Padilla

"THE CHANGING WALL"

NARRATOR   Jenny and Cloe both thought that the other's
life was so much more glamorous than their own. Jenny was a
millionaire with everything she ever wanted, like a cute dog
and a cute boyfriend. Cloe had enough money to get by, but her
parents were less protective than Jenny's. The two girls just
got out of school.

CLOE   Come on, Jenny! Let's go!

JENNY   (crying) Oh, well, Ben just broke up with me,
so stop nagging! I'm feeling horrible.

CLOE   Well, I'm not having such a great day either!

JENNY   Why? What happened?

CLOE   I just tanked my math test. Now my mom is going
to ground me into the next century!

JENNY   I'm sorry. Maybe you should study more?

CLOE   Hey, want to try something?

NARRATOR   Mary, Cloe's little sister, suddenly appears on
the scene.

MARY   What's that? I want to try something!

CLOE   Mary, go home!

        (CLOE points in the direction of her house.)

MARY   No! I want to go with you, or else I'm
telling mom!

CLOE   NO! GO!

        (MARY walks away, headed for her house.)

NARRATOR   Mary unwillingly left and headed for her house.
Little did Cloe know that Mary would be lurking in the bushes.

JENNY   So, where are we going?

CLOE   Shhh! Somewhere special. But I have one
important question to ask you.

JENNY   What?

CLOE   Do you want to switch bodies?

JENNY   What do you mean? You're crazy! Isn't that,
like, impossible?

NARRATOR   Cloe explained that when she was a child, her
grandfather had told her about the Changing Wall, a secret
wall that was used to relieve military charges. It could be
used when you were accused of something bad, but you had done
nothing of the sort. A loyal friend or kind general would
either take the blame and die for you, or try to convince the
people that you were innocent of whatever you were accused of
doing. But Cloe had a different, more diabolical reason, for
switching bodies with Jenny.

CLOE   Here we are. This is the changing wall. My
grandfather explained to me that it was a magical wall to
switch bodies.

JENNY   Whoa. Wait. How come you wanna switch bodies?

NARRATOR   Cloe smiled nervously and walked toward the
wall, touching it softly.

CLOE   I thought it would be fun.

JENNY   Okay. But will it really work?

        (CLOE and JENNY raise themselves to the top of the wall.)

CLOE   I don't know, I've never tried it before.
Careful, this wall is a little unstable. Okay, so we are on the
top and now … Jump!

NARRATOR   Jenny and Cloe jumped off of the top of the
Changing Wall, and the next thing they knew, they were in each
other's bodies, hugging happily. But then, Cloe (in Jenny's
body) disappeared!

JENNY   Cloe? Cloe? Cloe, where are you? Cloe? Cloe?
(sobbing) Cloe! Come back!

NARRATOR   Mary had seen the whole thing, but hadn't seen
where her sister went either.

MARY   Jenny? Where did Cloe… Ahhhh!

NARRATOR   Cloe, in Jenny's body, came up behind Jenny,
tied her up, then made her sit against the Changing Wall. She
smiled an evil smile. But then she saw her sister, and the
smile disappeared.

MARY   Cloe? How could you do that to your best friend?!

CLOE   Shh! This is only between you and me! It's a
good thing Jenny and I looked alike. Nobody has to know what
happened to her, so keep your mouth shut about it.

NARRATOR   Mary ran as fast as she could back to her
house, where she found her mother reading in the den. She was
panting for breath and scared.

MARY   Mom! Mom! Where are you?

MOM   I'm in the den.

MARY   I need to talk to you privately.

NARRATOR   Then Cloe bursts into the room, sweaty and tired.

MOM   Hi Jenny. Where's Cloe? What are you doing
here? Mary, come here sweetie. What's wrong? You look like
you've seen a ghost.

MARY   No, Mom! That's *Cloe*!

MOM   What? What are you talking about? That's *Jenny*.

CLOE   Yeah, what's wrong with you? I'm *Jenny*!

MARY   NO! You're not! You're not!

NARRATOR   Mary was speechless. She didn't know what to say.

MOM   Girls, stop it. Do you want some tea?

CLOE   Sure, Mrs. Brown. We'll be right back. Mary?
Can I speak with you upstairs?

MOM   Okay, I'll put the kettle on.

MARY   I… I… Okay.

NARRATOR   The girls glided upstairs and their mom turned
on the kettle, thinking, "What's wrong with those girls?"

CLOE   Mary, you better keep your mouth shut about
this! I'm gonna try my best to look like myself. Well, my real
self. And we are gonna live our lives normally as if nothing
happened.

MARY   I don't know if it's gonna work, but okay. But
answer one question.

CLOE   Okay. What?

MARY   Why did you do it?

CLOE   Do what?

MARY   You know, what you did to Jenny.

CLOE   Oh. I... I always knew I was better than Jenny.
She was always stuck-up and mean! I hated her! Even though she
was my best friend forever. BFF!

          (CLOE laughs an evil laugh.)

MARY   How evil. I can't believe you would do that!

CLOE   I know! I'm proud of myself.

          (CLOE laughs again. She walks away and waves goodbye
to MARY.)

Vadim Merenosvskiy

"GHOST"

NARRATOR   It was sunny and cool because it was fall.
Yoh and Manta were walking to school. They were thinking about
Halloween, and what they going to wear. When they got to
school, they went into their classroom.

TEACHER   Sit down. I have an announcement to make.

          (Everyone gets excited.)

TEACHER   We are going to the movie theater for Halloween!

STUDENTS   Cool!

TEACHER   On Halloween, there will be no school, so we
have to meet somewhere.

MANTA   How about at school?

YOH   Or at the theater?

TEACHER   We are going to meet at the theater at six p.m.
on Halloween day, but for now, let's get back to work.

NARRATOR   Everyone got excited. When school ended,
everyone ran out the doors. The last ones were Manta and Yoh.
They were quiet because they were thinking about something.
They were quiet until they came to the river. They stopped and
lay down on the grass.

YOH   Is that cool to go to the movie theater?

MANTA   Yeah, but what kind of movie are we going to
watch?

YOH   About ghosts, I think.

MANTA   I am not going, then.

YOH   Are you scared of ghosts?

MANTA   I am kind of scared of ghosts.

YOH   They aren't real! I haven't seen one.

MANTA   I know but they're creepy and scary. I had a
scary dream.

YOH   Don't worry, it will be fun!

NARRATOR   They lay for an hour and went home. The next
day, everyone was so excited because the next day was movie
day. The students in the classroom didn't even pay attention
to the teacher, so she let them play outside all day.

MANTA   Are you excited?

YOH   Are you?

MANTA   Well… I asked first!

YOH   Actually, I am.

MANTA   I am not really that excited because I am
scared of ghosts.

YOH   Okay, let go to the park and play there.

MANTA   Okay, let's go.

NARRATOR   The day went fast, and everyone was still
excited about the movies. The next day, at six p.m. they all
met at the theater. They went in, and sat down, and the movie
started. After thirty minutes, they got to a part where a ghost
appeared in the movie, and everyone got scared. But at that
moment, a real ghost looked down from the ceiling. He went
behind the movie screen, and then jumped out of the screen!
Everyone got scared and ran out of the building. Only Yoh and
Manta stayed behind. They looked the ghost and the ghost looked
at them. Manta was scared and Yoh was calm.

GHOST   Are you scared?

YOH   Not really.

MANTA	Of course we are!
GHOST	Then why didn't you run away?
MANTA	I don't know.
YOH	Do you live here?
GHOST	Sometimes, why?
YOH	Do you want to be friends?
MANTA & GHOST	What?
MANTA	No way!
YOH	Why not?
GHOST	I never had a friend before.
YOH	We don't have a ghost friend.
GHOST	No.
MANTA	So what? Let's get out of here!
YOH	Really, you don't want to be our friend?
GHOST	Well, okay. My name is Amedamary.

YOH   I'm Yoh and he is Manta, and I think that our class has left because you scared them. I am going out to find my class.

MANTA   I think that our class probably called the cops!

YOH   Can you turn invisible and come with us? The we can get this problem fixed right away.

NARRATOR   When they got outside, there were cops and their teacher and some of their classmates.

TEACHER   Are you okay?

YOH   Are you sure you are okay? I think that the movie gave you an illusion!

TEACHER   No, but how about going trick or treating now?

STUDENTS   Yeah!

AMEDAMARY   So where am I going to live now?

YOH   You are going to live in my house!

MANTA   But please don't scare me.

AMEDAMARY   Okay, but no guarantee.

MANTA   What do you mean no guarantee?

AMEDAMARY   Okay, I am not going to scare you.

MANTA   Thanks so much!

NARRATOR   They went home down the long, black street.
But Amedamary did start scaring Manta, until Yoh yelled at him
to stop.

45.

"YELLOW"

(CHRISTY is asleep. She wakes up. Everything around her is yellow. She rubs her eyes, yawns, opens her eyes, but she is still half-asleep. She looks around, squinting, and rubs her eyes a second time. Her eyes widen. She vigorously shakes her head.)

CHRISTY   Whu-u-u-t? (Pause) Jesus, is there something wrong with my eyes?

(CHRISTY runs toward DANNY's room.)

CHRISTY   Why is everything yellow?! (to DANNY) You little brat, what did you do to my eyes?

(DANNY makes plane noises and glides a toy plane around. He doesn't hear CHRISTY.)

DANNY   Vrrrrrrr … vrrrrrrr!

(CHRISTY screams.)

CHRISTY   O-M-G!

DANNY   Vrrrrrr!

CHRISTY   You're yellow too!

(CHRISTY jumps up and down frantically, waving her hands in front of Danny's face.)

CHRISTY   Helloooo? Can you hear me?

(DANNY gets up and glides his plane around the room. Suddenly, he falls over and starts crying.)

DANNY   Mommy! Mommy!

CHRISTY   (hysterical) Am I dreaming?

        (She breathes deeply, trying to calm down, keeping one
hand on her chest. She speaks to an oblivious DANNY.)

CHRISTY   Please tell me I'm dreaming!

DANNY   (yelling) MOMMY!!

CHRISTY   (thinking to herself) This is just a really
lame nightmare. Yes. Yes!

        (CHRISTY holds a finger in the air.)

CHRISTY   This is just a really lame nightmare about the
ugly color yellow!

        (CHRISTY starts pacing back and forth.)

CHRISTY   No, wait… what if… what if I'm going crazy?
(Pause) what if I'm seeing things?

        (She runs her hands though her hair.)

CHRISTY   No, no! This can't be!

        (MOM runs into the room. She soothes DANNY.)

MOM   Danny? Oh, Danny. Shh, shh, stop crying, deary.

        (CHRISTY panics again, suddenly realizing that MOM is
in the room.)

CHRISTY   Mom!! Mom! Help, what's going on?

        (She runs up to her, her head down, and she hugs MOM.)

CHRISTY   Mom, Mom, Mom! Everything looks yellow. What's
going on? What's happening?

        (MOM is still hugging DANNY, moving like CHRISTY is not
hugging her.)

CHRISTY   Mom?

        (MOM looks up, but does not hear CHRISTY.)

MOM   Hmm. I wonder if Christy is still sleeping.
I better get her out of bed soon.

        (CHRISTY looks up, then immediately pulls back, and she
starts crying.)

CHRISTY   Mom, you're yellow too, and you can't hear me
either! I am here!

        (CHRISTY looks at her arm and screams, holding out both
her arms. She watches yellow colors creep through her arms,
slowly swallowing her natural color. She stomps both feet,
running in place.)

CHRISTY   NOO!

        (She runs to the hallway, vigorously trying to scrub
the yellow that is creeping over her body.)

CHRISTY   I'm going crazy! When will this nightmare end?

        (She tries to calm herself, talking in a slow measured
voice. She stops scrubbing her arms.)

CHRISTY   Ok, I'm going to go back to bed, and go back to
sleep. and I will wake up normal.

        (CHRISTY closes her eyes and smiles. She opens her eyes
slowly as she walks back to her room, climbs into the bed and
pulls the covers over her head.)

CHRISTY   Okay, I'm going to count to three, and then I
WILL wake up normal, and everyone will see me! Yes. Yes, that
will happen! Okay. 1, 2, 3!

(CHRISTY looks up.)

CHRISTY   No! Come on, this has to work!

          (CHRISTY breathes out loudly. She pulls the covers over
her head. She exhales.)

CHRISTY   Okay! 1, 2, 3.

          (CHRISTY looks around, and pounds her fists into the
blanket.)

CHRISTY   No! No! No! No! I'll never leave this horrible
dream!

          (CHRISTY pulls her pillow over her head firmly,
screaming and kicking her legs.)

Elias Mohamed Hassan
Eliezer Marquez Geronimo

"THE DRAGON SLAYER"

*Publisher's Note: These authors chose to begin their work by
creating a story. Now they'd like to invite you to imagine it
as a play!*

One night forty-five men were trying to save the princess.
One by one they got burned or eaten by the dragons. Some
dragons got killed, but the men left one dragon, that was the
queen. The men were all killed by the queen dragon. Ten years
later a soldier got news and told Jeff to come and rescue the
princess. Jeff asked his younger brother, Troy, if he should go
to save the princess.

"I could help you if you want to fight the dragon," Troy said.

"Yes," said Jeff.

Troy said, "Should we rescue her today?"

"I need to buy a sword and a shield," Jeff said.

Troy wondered how old the princess was. Back when the
soldiers were killed, Troy was ten years old. Jeff was twenty
years old. And Stephanie, the princess, was thirty years old.
Troy thought to himself, "Where is the castle?"

Jeff and Troy walked for five days and five nights. They
tried to find a cave to sleep in. They found a dead deer, and
they cooked it and ate it. The next day they moved on. They
found villages, and they asked for the Hero Castle.

Two days later, they could see the castle on a big hill. Troy heard the dragon roar. Jeff took out some binoculars, and he saw the princess in a huge tower. Jeff saw a horse. Jeff told Troy to catch it. Troy took out a rope and put it on the horse.

"You think it's trained?" said Jeff. "It ran away from the castle."

"How do you know that?" said Troy. There was horse armor on the ground.

"Let's put the armor on him to get to the castle faster, and we will save the princess!"

"Good luck, brother!" said Jeff.

"You too!" said Troy.

They got to the castle. There were bones everywhere. Troy knew the weak spot of the dragon. They saw the princess. She said, "Behind you!"

"Run!" said Jeff.

"Her weak spot is her tail!" said Troy. Jeff hit the dragon on her tail fifty-five times. She was dying and he ran with Troy to the top of the castle. The princess was safe.

The queen dragon was so big that she hit the tower when she died. Troy fell down but Jeff did not know Troy fell. Jeff got the princess, but when he turned around, Troy wasn't there! Troy was dead.

Jeff and the princess got to the stairs, but they were broken. Jeff took Troy and the princess. They got home and Jeff buried Troy in the sand. Jeff and the princess lived happily ever after.

Chapter 3

Relationships

Adam Mascheri
Manuel Loya

"THE BREAK UP"

(SAMANTHA's house, after school, 6 p.m. SLAPPY enters the nice living room.)

SLAPPY   I hate you!

SAMANTHA   But why?

SLAPPY   You know why!

SAMANTHA   Why?

SLAPPY   Don't play that stupid game with me!

        (SLAPPY sighs.)

SLAPPY   Well my friend Mike told me you've been kissing someone else.

SAMANTHA   But I didn...

SLAPPY   Yes, you did! Mike told me you did it, so don't tell me those little crappy lies that you tell.

SAMANTHA   Mike? He always tells lies.

SLAPPY   Well, I should know that if he does. I've known him since the first grade and he has never told me lies.

SAMANTHA   Well, you believed him in first grade because you were a stupid little brat then. Are you going to believe him or me?

SLAPPY   Well I...

SAMANTHA   You what?

SLAPPY   Um, sorry?

SAMANTHA   Sorry! That's all you have to say to me, after you thought that I kissed another guy! He probably told you that so he could try to go out with me.

SLAPPY   But I…

SAMANTHA   But what, huh? I hate you too then!

(SAMANTHA exits and slams the door.)

(Morning, the next day, SLAPPY's house.)

(SLAPPY is munching on a bowl of Cocoa Krispies next to his brother FRED.)

SLAPPY   (mouthful) I'm going to breakup with Samantha.

FRED   What?

(SLAPPY swallows cereal.)

SLAPPY   I'm going to break up with Samantha.

FRED   But why would you breakup with Samantha? She's super fine and really nice.

SLAPPY   Well, I know that, but we had a fight last night.

FRED   I didn't hear anything.

SLAPPY   That's because we weren't here, dummy!

FRED   Oh yeah. What were you fighting about?

(Later that day, at Roosevelt High School.)

SAMANTHA   (looking away) Hey.

SLAPPY   (hopeful) Hey!

FRED   Hey, Samantha! How ya doin'?

SAMANTHA   Fine.

(She sighs, dejected.)

FRED   Why so droopy?

SAMANTHA   Well, why don't you ask your-

        (Bell rings.)

        (After school.)

SLAPPY   Hey Samantha, meet me at the flagpole at three
o'clock!

SAMANTHA   (hesitantly) Okay.

        (SLAPPY and SAMANTHA walk away in opposite directions.)

        (FRED and SLAPPY meet in front of the school. SLAPPY
walks over to FRED and closes his phone.)

SLAPPY   Hey Fred, mom just called and said she wanted
you home.

FRED   Why didn't she call me on my phone?

SLAPPY   She said you weren't picking up.

        (FRED checks his phone.)

FRED   I don't have any missed calls.

SLAPPY   If I give you ten dollars, will you go home?

FRED   No, and why do you want me...

SLAPPY   Just go to the football field and wait for
ten minutes!

FRED   FINE!!!

        (FRED stomps away. SLAPPY approaches the hottest girls
in eleventh grade and tells them to circle around FRED for ten
dollars each. They agree. SLAPPY goes to the flagpole.)

SAMANTHA   Where have you been? I've been waiting for
ten minutes!

SLAPPY   Sorry, Fred was being a pain. I...

          (FRED runs towards SLAPPY, his arms flailing.)

FRED   STOOOOPP!!

          (FRED runs into SLAPPY's arm as he raises it.)

SLAPPY   Oops!! (chuckle)

FRED   (groggily) Oooooohhhhhh. (pause) What are you
guys doing? Don't you remember you used to love each other?

SLAPPY   You know Fred, you're right. Samantha,
I love you.

SAMANTHA   I love you too.

          (SAMANTHA and SLAPPY hug.)

FRED   EEEEWWWWWWW!!!!!

          (SLAPPY hits FRED and knocks him out.)

Quan Lou
Judy He
Thao Nguyen

"THE FRIENDSHIP"

      (It is two weeks into the new school year. <u>LAUREN</u> and <u>HELEN</u> see <u>KARIN</u> approaching them in the hallway.)

<u>LAUREN</u>   Why are you so happy?

<u>KARIN</u>   I just met a boy!

<u>HELEN</u>   What's his name?

<u>KARIN</u>   His name is Nick, and he is really handsome.

<u>HELEN</u>   What? Nick who?

<u>KARIN</u>   The guy who was in the same gym class with me!

      (<u>HELEN</u>'s face turns red.)

<u>LAUREN</u>   What's going on, Helen? How come your face just turned so red?

<u>KARIN</u>   Are you okay?

<u>HELEN</u>   Oh! Nothing. I just remembered I have something I need to do. So, see you guys later.

      (<u>HELEN</u> runs to the bathroom, crying.)

<u>LAUREN</u>   What happened to her? There must be something wrong with her.

<u>KARIN</u>   I have no idea what's up with her. That was really weird.

(After school, <u>HELEN</u> comes home later than usual and goes straight to her room to avoid talking to her family members. Soon, the phone rings.)

LAUREN   Hello? Is Helen there? This is Lauren.

HELEN   Hi, Lauren. It's me.

LAUREN   Where did you go? Karin and I were looking for you all over the school and we couldn't find you.

HELEN   Umm, I was in the bathroom because I had a stomach problem.

LAUREN   Are you feeling better now?

HELEN   Yeah. I'm okay. Were you worried about me?

LAUREN   Of course, but what happened?

          (<u>HELEN</u> starts to sob.)

LAUREN   Are you crying? What's wrong, Helen? You can talk to me. I'm really worried about you.

HELEN   Well, I became very sad when Karin told us that she likes Nick.

LAUREN   So what? You should be happy for her. Why do you have to cry?

HELEN   I'm crying because...

LAUREN   Because why?

HELEN   Because I like Nick, too.

LAUREN   Wha... What?

HELEN   I knew I shouldn't have told you about it!

LAUREN   Of course you should have. We are best
friends, right?

HELEN   Yeah. But somehow I feel stupid.

LAUREN   Why do you feel stupid?

HELEN   Well, if both Karin and I like the same guy,
that can create some problem.

LAUREN   But if you like someone, no one can change your
feelings. It's just how you feel.

HELEN   I know, but I'm afraid if she finds it out,
she may not want to talk to me ever again.

LAUREN   Don't' be ridiculous. Karin wouldn't do that.
I think you should just tell her how you feel about Nick.

HELEN   Really? Well, would you come with me when I
tell her about it?

LAUREN   Sure. I think everything is gonna be okay.

          (The next day HELEN reveals to KARIN that she also likes
NICK. Later that day, KARIN tells NICK that HELEN likes him. NICK
tries to convince KARIN to stop being friends with HELEN because
NICK doesn't like HELEN. KARIN struggles to accept his suggestion,
but eventually she decides to choose NICK over HELEN.)

KARIN   Helen, I need to speak with you.

HELEN   Sure, what is it?

KARIN   Well, to be frank, I really don't want to be
friends with you anymore.

HELEN   But why? Wait! Karin, wait!

          (KARIN turns around and runs away, leaving HELEN
shocked and alone in the hallway. HELEN starts to sob as she
slowly walks back to her classroom.)

LAUREN   Helen, are you okay?

HELEN   Karin told me that she doesn't want to be
friends with me anymore!

LAUREN   WHAT? We've been best friends for such a long
time! She can't treat her best friend this way. That's just
wrong!

HELEN   It must be because I told her about my feelings
for Nick.

LAUREN   Oh, Helen! I'm sure it'll all work out fine.

          (After school, LAUREN and HELEN go to a nearby park to
talk. They see NICK walking through the park with another girl.)

HELEN   Lauren, did you see that? They were holding
hands!

LAUREN   I thought Karin was supposed to be the one
holding Nick's hand.

HELEN   I know! Should we tell Karin about it?

LAUREN   I think we should.

          (LAUREN and HELEN go to KARIN's house. KARIN answers
the door.)

LAUREN   Hi Karin. There is something we thought you
should know. We were at the park after school and saw Nick
walking with a girl, and they were holding hands! We don't
really think Nick is such a nice guy, after all.

KARIN   Well, actually, I've heard some rumors, too.

HELEN   We just didn't want you to be hurt.

KARIN   Oh. Thanks, guys. Well, Helen, I said some mean
things to you earlier today. I'm really sorry.

HELEN   That's all right. I'm just happy that we can be
friends again.

LAUREN   We have been best friends forever!

LAUREN, KARIN, & HELEN   And we will be best friends forever!

Amy Acevedo
Maria Garcia
Fatuma Mahmud

"THE SUSPENSION"

(JAZMIN and BANANA walk into PRINCIPAL CHARLES CHUCKY CHARMING's office.)

MR. CHARMING   Take a seat, Mr. Banana and Ms. Jazmin. Why were you both screaming on the stairs? I heard you all the way from my office.

(BANANA and JAZMIN speak at the same time.)

BANANA & JAZMIN   It wasn't me.

MR. CHARMING   One at the time.

BANANA   I was in the bathroom, and when I came into class, Ms. Computer was screaming. She was asking, "Who did it?" Jazmin said that it was me. Ms. Computer didn't know that I was in the bathroom, because she was on her computer and didn't know where I was.

MR. CHARMING   Okay, but first, why were you out of the classroom? And why didn't Ms. Computer know where you were?

BANANA   I came to school late, and went straight to the bathroom. Then I went to my locker, and forgot to get a pass to class.

(MR. CHARMING turns to JAZMIN.)

MR. CHARMING   If Banana wasn't in the classroom, then why do you think he did it?

JAZMIN   Banana came into the class with scissors in one hand and a hall pass in the other. Maestra Computadora was checking her email, y Banana came up behind her and cut her hair. Don't believe him. No le crea siempre se mete en problemas. He is always lying and getting suspended! He lies about everything he does.

BANANA   No, I don't lie, but I do get suspended a lot of times.

JAZMIN   He is always getting in trouble, and always doing stuff a los maestros.

MR. CHARMING   We're going to get to the bottom of this. I am going to call Ms. Computer to see what she has to say about this.

          (MR. CHARMING picks up the phone.)

MR. CHARMING   It's Mr. Charming. I have two of your students down here in the office with me. And I wanted to ask you if you knew where Banana was during the incident?

          (MR. CHARMING nods his head and hangs up. He turns to BANANA.)

MR. CHARMING   Ms. Computer didn't know where you were because she was checking her e-mails. She was on her computer the whole time.

BANANA   I told you! I came late to school, and went to the bathroom, and forgot a pass, and had to get out my scissors to cut a paper.

          (MR. CHARMING turns to BANANA with an angry face.)

MR. CHARMING   So you did cut her hair?

JAZMIN   See, I told you. El lo hizo.

MR. CHARMING   Banana, you did it! We have proof, and you will be suspended.

JAZMIN   I told you that he lies about todo.

MR. CHARMING   You will go home or we can call your parents so
that they can come have a meeting.

BANANA   Pero, I didn't do anything wrong. Tell me,
what's the proof?

JAZMIN   I found these pieces of white hair on your
desk. So you can't lie anymore.

BANANA   What? Oh no. Please, please don't call my
parents.

MR. CHARMING   Well, that's what I am going to have to do.
Sorry. Next time you won't do such a horrible thing to someone.

          (JAZMIN walks away while BANANA and MR. CHARMING remain
in the office.)

August Wolgamott

"THE BREAK UP"

(CHLOE and ISAAC meet at school.)

CHLOE   Hey, wanna go get something to eat? ...and will Joseph be coming by any chance?

ISAAC   Of course I do! And maybe it should just be the two of us. I haven't seen you in a long time! I miss it just being the two of us!

CHLOE   Oh, okay. Well, I just figured maybe you would want to bring him. I mean, I really miss us all hanging out. We used to all be, like, best friends!

ISAAC   Well, maybe you are right. I miss hanging out, all three of us, as well. So, maybe Joseph will come. Does that sound like fun, all three of us? Because I also miss it, and I miss you. So whatever makes you happy!

CHLOE   Yes, that sounds great! Pick me up after you get Joe! Tonight will be fun! Seven or eight o'clock!

ISAAC   Okay! Sounds like a plan. But some night we need to hang out, just the two of us!

CHLOE   Okay, well I gotta go get ready. I'll talk to you later! Don't forget to call Joe and pick him up on the way to my hou...

ISAAC   Okay, okay. Bye!

(End Scene)

(ISAAC honks his car horn. CHLOE runs to the car.)

ISAAC   Hey Chloe! (He gives her a kiss.) Sorry I'm a
little late!

   (CHLOE turns around and hugs JOSEPH.)

CHLOE   Hey Joseph!

   (ISAAC is confused.)

JOSEPH   Hey Chloe, Long time no see. How have you been?

CHLOE   I know! I have been good, and yourself?

ISAAC   Chloe, are you mad at me? What's wrong? No
hello to me?

   (CHLOE ignores ISAAC.)

JOSEPH   Glad to hear it. I have been great as well!

CHLOE   Good! So what have you been trying to say to
me, Isaac?

ISAAC   Never mind!

   (End Scene)

CHLOE   So… Let's eat!

ISAAC & JOSEPH   Yes! Let's eat!

ISAAC   But first, I need to go to the restroom.

CHLOE & JOSEPH   Okay, hurry back!

CHLOE   I… umm… like you… umm… a lot.

   (JOSEPH kisses CHLOE. She kisses back. They start to
make out. ISSAC leaves the bathroom, and starts walking back
to the table. CHLOE and JOSEPH stop kissing, wipe their faces
clean, and sit nervously, pretending to have a conversation.)

ISAAC   What the heck is this?!

CHLOE & JOSEPH Uh, Nothing. Everything is fine.

ISAAC   I'm leaving... I need time to think about this...
everything is going wrong! I need some time... I will talk to
you two later!

        (End Scene)

ISAAC   Hello?

CHLOE   Hi...

ISAAC   We need to...

CHLOE   TALK! I know. Why did you leave last night?!

ISAAC   I don't think...

CHLOE   You don't think what?!

ISAAC   I don't think we... we... we can be together
anymore!

CHLOE   Why?! Is it because of last night?

ISAAC   No!

CHLOE   It is... I know it! He kissed me first!

ISAAC   It doesn't matter who kissed who...

CHLOE   So then why...

ISAAC   Because!

CHLOE   Because why?! I'm sorry for what I did... It was
a HUGE mistake! Really!

ISAAC   Okay... but Chloe...

CHLOE   WHAT?!

ISAAC   (Yelling) OUR PARENTS!

CHLOE   Screw them! (Pause.) Wait... what about them?!

ISAAC   They're... Umm...

CHLOE   WHAT!?

ISAAC   THEY'RE GETTING MARRIED!

CHLOE   Wait... your dad? And my mom? (Pause.) So?

ISAAC   We are going to be related! Our parents are
going to be married... we are going to be living together... if
we were going out, it just wouldn't be a good idea! You know?
Because... it just... isn't smart!

CHLOE   I guess. I guess you're right.

          (End Scene)

CHLOE   My mom is getting married to Isaac's dad!
My mom is getting married to Isaac's dad! My mom is getting
married to Isaac's dad! OH NO!

          (The phone rings. CHLOE picks it up.)

ISAAC   Hey Chloe!

          (CHLOE is not in the mood to be speaking on the phone.)

CHLOE   Hi.

CHLOE & ISAAC So I was thinking... (Pause)... About?

CHLOE   You go first!

ISAAC   Okay... We need to break...

CHLOE   Up! I know!

ISAAC   So... we're broken up right?!

CHLOE   Yeah... I love you... Bro...

Brier Cross

"THE OTHER WAY HOME"

(BOB and JOE walk out of a movie theater. JOE is
holding a flashlight.)

BOB   That was a good movie, wasn't it?

JOE   Yeah, it was!

BOB   Which way do you think we should go home?

JOE   Let's go the usual way home.

BOB   Nah, lets go the other way home today.

JOE   I don't think that's a good idea.

BOB   C'mon you wimp!

JOE   I really don't think we should go that way!

BOB   It'll be fun.

JOE   I've got the flashlight, so we're going this
way. Or don't you remember you told me that you're afraid of
the dark?

        (BOB grabs flashlight away from JOE.)

BOB   Now I've got the flashlight, so we're going
this way!

JOE   Fine!

        (JOE mutters under his breath.)

BOB   What was that?

JOE   Nothing.

(JOE and BOB are walking down the street. They stop. There is a BUM sitting on the curb.)

BUM   Alms for the poor!

BOB   Why would we give our money to you? What have you done for us?

BUM   Please, man, I just need some money.

BOB   No.

JOE   I really don't think we should be out here!

BOB   Why? We've got a flashlight, don't we?

JOE   Yes, but what if someone jumps out of the shadows and shoots our heads off?

(BOB grabs JOE and slaps him.)

BOB   Snap out of it! What are the chances of that?

JOE   I'd say pretty good, judging by where we are!

(BOB grabs JOE and slaps him again.)

BOB   I told you to snap out of it.

JOE   I'm not going to take that from you.

(JOE punches BOB in the face.)

BOB   Oh, that was the last straw.

(BOB punches JOE in the stomach.)

JOE   Oh, heck no!

       (JOE punches BOB in the kidney.)

       (BOB grabs JOE's head and smashes it against his own. They both collapse, dazed.)

       (BUM walks up and steals their wallets. He tried to sneak off, but JOE looks up.)

JOE   Stop thief!

       (JOE and BOB chase after the BUM. They knock him down and get their wallets back.)

BOB   We probably could have handled that differently.

JOE   Probably.

BOB   Joe, I'm sorry about what I said back there.

JOE   Me too.

BOB   Friends?

JOE   Friends.

Arianna Huertas
Veronica Johanson

"WE'RE GONNA MAKE IT"

(Brothers <u>AUSTIN</u> and <u>EVAN</u> meet their friend <u>DARREN</u> in the main school hallway of Berkley High School.)

<u>DARREN</u>   Hey guys, what class are you heading to now?

<u>AUSTIN</u>   I'm on my way to the best class there is...
(cough, cough)

<u>EVAN</u> & <u>DARREN</u>   Gym?

(<u>AUSTIN</u> looks at <u>DARREN</u> and <u>EVAN</u> as if they were psychic. He looks at his muscles and kisses them.)

<u>AUSTIN</u>   I think these babies need a little work out.

(<u>EVAN</u> looks away and changes the subject.)

<u>EVAN</u>   Hey, I saw these guys who looked like they were from the Army. They were wearing uniforms and there was a black Hummer out in front of the school. It was pretty cool.

<u>DARREN</u>   Yeah right, you little liar! Where?

<u>AUSTIN</u>   They were heading out to the front of the building, I saw them, too. They were in the main hallway heading out. It wasn't that cool, Evan.

<u>EVAN</u>   Whatever, Austin. What do you think they were here for?

(<u>DARREN</u> shrugs and backs up, looking at <u>EVAN</u>.)

DARREN   I don't even want to know. If it's one of those break-in things again, I'm out of here. Those schemes are so stupid. People need to stop pulling those pranks; it's a waste of time.

EVAN   Uhmmm... okay? Austin, what do you think they were here for?

DARREN   Evan, shut up. I just hope I don't have to do anything with it.

AUSTIN   Hey, I bet everyone has to do with it.

DARREN   Well, let's just hope it's not another scheme again.

(Bell rings.)

EVAN   See you later guys, I got to get to...

(He looks at AUSTIN and makes fun of him.)

..."the best class there is"... MATH.

(AUSTIN nods his head and squints his eyes angrily at EVAN while he walks away. DARREN leans toward AUSTIN.)

DARREN   Just let it go man...

AUSTIN   I'm sick and tired of that punk. Seriously...

DARREN   Well, I'll uh... See you later.

(DARREN walks to his science class and AUSTIN is still staring into space. He glances at the red lockers and punches one to get his anger out. He looks at the clock and walks to class.)

(Later...)

(AUSTIN, EVAN and DARREN meet in the main hallway again. AUSTIN is over what EVAN did and tries to ignore it.)

DARREN   Well, that was a waste of time.

          (EVAN looks at his watch.)

EVAN   Yeah, I'm thinking about changing my schedule
soon. My locker is on the first floor and my second, third,
fourth, fifth and sixth periods are all on the fourth floor. It
sucks.

          (AUSTIN looks over EVAN's shoulder and sees a poster.
He stares at it for a second and walks over to it. EVAN gets
out of his way.)

AUSTIN   What's this? This must be why those Army men
were here.

          (DARREN and AUSTIN look behind them and DARREN reads
the poster.)

DARREN   Join the Army and fight for your country. Join
by November 30th.

AUSTIN   Hey, that's not a bad idea. I've always wanted
to join the Army. It just sounds so cool. What do you say Darren?

          (DARREN looks at AUSTIN as if he were crazy.)

EVAN   Yeah, Darren, we should go. It will be cool
with all the bombs, guns, and tanks… all the technology
they've got.

          (DARREN looks at EVAN as if he were crazy, and AUSTIN
stares at EVAN as if he were the dumbest person on the planet.)

AUSTIN   Evan… You are such a geek, I swear man. All
you ever think about is technology and math and science. Just
shut up! Danggg.

EVAN   Well, I don't go around showing off my
tiny muscles!

AUSTIN   Whatever, Evan, you're just mad because you

don't have any. All you have are brains!

(EVAN ignores AUSTIN and looks at DARREN, who is standing there watching them argue.)

DARREN   Are you guys crazy? The war!? You'll kill yourselves out there!

(EVAN chuckles.)

AUSTIN   Calm down, D, you should join with us.

DARREN   Umm... I'm okay. Are you guys seriously going to join though? You know, there's a forty-five percent chance you'll live.

(AUSTIN and EVAN look at each other. They grab a form and put their names on the sign up list as DARREN watches them. DARREN looks confused.)

AUSTIN   So you going to join or what? Don't just stand there. Man up!

(EVAN thinks for a second and looks at DARREN.)

EVAN   You know how you said there was a forty-five percent chance you'll live? Well, it's actually a thirty-seven percent chance...

AUSTIN   Evan?

EVAN   What?

AUSTIN   SHUT UP.

(EVAN rolls his eyes at AUSTIN and turns toward DARREN.)

EVAN   So why don't you want to join? I mean, no pressure, but there is only a month left.

DARREN   I don't know. I've had some experiences, guys. I don't think I can go.

AUSTIN   Experiences? Like what?

DARREN   Did you ever meet my dad?

EVAN   Your dad? Didn't he, like, move away to Australia or something?

AUSTIN   Evan, what are you talking about? You've never met him before.

          (He turns toward DARREN.)

          I think you told me about him, like, two years ago, but I don't really remember what you said.

DARREN   You remember when I told you? Well, he was in the Army, too. You get the picture?

EVAN   So, where's he now?

DARREN   He passed away two years ago. He was saving his best friend, but I guess he died too. Some plane dropped a bomb a couple of feet away from them. At least that's what I heard. I don't like to talk about it with my mom because I don't know how she would react.

AUSTIN   Dang, bro, I'm sorry. I didn't know...

EVAN   Is that why you don't want to go or something?

DARREN   Kind of. If I go... I could end up like my dad. But if I don't... you guys...

EVAN   Darren, even though I have never been through that experience, I know how you feel.

AUSTIN   Yeah, just know that we'll always be there for you, no matter what.

DARREN   Yeah, same with me.

          (The bell rings. AUSTIN and EVAN give a little tap on

DARREN's shoulder. They glance at the poster and walk away.
DARREN looks at the clock and jogs to his next class.)

EVAN   Dude, think about what Darren said... What if?

AUSTIN   Evan, I'm going to join no matter what Darren
says! It's my decision and he can deal with his own problems
right now! And if you don't want to join, that's fine with me!
I just wanna be able to go there and come back!

EVAN   I'm just saying... Of course I want to go, cause
you're my brother. But that doesn't mean we should leave out
our best friend! How do you think he feels?!

AUSTIN   Yeah, but what about how I feel, or how I
think?! Does any of that matter to you since I'm your brother?!

EVAN   Of course it matters! But it's not always about
you! Darren has twice the problems you do right now! His father
died, okay? We're the only friends he's got, and we can't just
leave him behind.

AUSTIN   (pauses) I'm going to talk to Darren after class.

        (Later...)

AUSTIN   Darren, I need to talk to you.

DARREN   Yeah, sure. What's wrong?

AUSTIN   Evan and I were...

DARREN   Fighting?

AUSTIN   Well, that too, but I didn't really care about
what you said earlier today, until Evan made me realize that
you're going through a really tough decision.

DARREN   Yeah, it's tougher than it looks, but...

        (DARREN walks over to the poster and signs his name on
the sign-up sheet and takes a form. EVAN arrives and watches.)

EVAN   Darren, what made you change your mind?

DARREN   You guys did. I never grew up with any siblings
to help me make the right choice. You guys are lucky to have
each other.

        (AUSTIN and EVAN look at each other.)

EVAN   We are pretty lucky, huh?

AUSTIN   Well, yeah. And Darren, you know you can always
come to us as if we were your brothers.

        (DARREN smiles and sticks his fist out.)

DARREN   We always have been...

        (AUSTIN and EVAN pound DARREN's fist.)

DARREN   And you know what, you guys? I'm not even going
to think about my dad right now. I'm gonna do it my way.

EVAN   And whether we make it or not, we'll always
have each other's backs.

        (DARREN looks over EVAN's shoulder at his red locker.)

DARREN   (frowning) Why is there a dent in my locker? It
wasn't there earlier. What the heck?!

        (He goes up and touches the dent.)

AUSTIN   Ummm, I don't know... Well... better go...

        (AUSTIN runs off, knowing it was him who punched
DARREN's locker earlier. DARREN looks at EVAN.)

DARREN   It was him, wasn't it?

EVAN   Probably...

        (They both smile and walk to class.)

Chloë Noonan

"COFFEE SHOP MADNESS"

(ALEX and RUBY are talking in a little coffee shop downtown. While ALEX and RUBY are talking, MELODY crashes into them while rushing to school.)

ALEX   Yowww! You'll need to pay for this!

RUBY   Alex, chill.

ALEX   (mumbles) Arggg!

MELODY   (confused) What?!

ALEX   (raging) Look what you did!

MELODY   I need to get to school. Bye.

ALEX   Slow down there. Look at what you did.
You spilled cocoa all over Ruby and me.

RUBY   Umm… I'm okay. I think you're overreacting
Alex. I know you. Just settle down.

MELODY   Yeah, I agree with her on that one. Okay, bye.

ALEX   No! Don't leave! You need to say sorry
or something!

MELODY   Uh, no I don't. You're sort of the one who
spilled the stupid drinks.

RUBY   Guys, calm down! You're both being rude.
Now what is your name?

MELODY   Melody.

RUBY   (to herself) Blah, blah, blah. Fight, fight,
fight is all they ever do.

ALEX   You know, you can be late to school. Are you
some dumb, straight-A student nerd thing? Or in a nerdy before-
school club?

MELODY   Are you some punkish, bully, mean person who
criticizes people?!

RUBY   Okay, that's it! I need a cocoa!

ALEX & MELODY   What?!

RUBY   (very loudly) I'm getting mad! You guys are
being ridiculous! One, why do you have to go to school in a
hurry? Two, Alex why are you screaming mean stuff at Melody?

MELODY   I need to get to school because I have a
before-school club... AND IT'S NOT NERDY!

ALEX   What is this before-school club you speak of?

RUBY   (confused) Whoa, whoa, whoa! Are you going to
criticize her club, Alex?

MELODY   That's it. I want to leave.

RUBY   (quickly) Melody. Stop! Come back here!

ALEX   I'm not done yet anyway. And if you need to go
to that before-school club of yours, you better go now but you
do need to apologize.

MELODY   I have to go to my book club every Tuesday.
And I needed to be there about six minutes ago.

RUBY   (giggles) It's Thursday.

ALEX   (giggles) No, it's Tuesday. Okay, run along
little Melody. Nice to…

RUBY   --No, it's Thursday.

ALEX & MELODY   I swear! It's Tuesday!

ALEX   (annoyed) Ruby, it's Tuesday and now Melody
is late for her book club group people thing. Now again I will
say, rush along dear Melody and goodbye.

RUBY   Alex, calm down.

        (RUBY, ALEX and MELODY move to a table and start
talking and arguing some more, without noticing that ALEX is
turning to MELODY's side of the new argument.)

RUBY   (angry) I know I'm right. Just look at your
calendar!

        (ALEX gives a confused look.)

RUBY   (sassy) Your cell phone? Doesn't it have a
calendar?

        (ALEX opens her phone and looks at the date. Her eyes
widen, her lips curl, her face turns red and she announces the
date.)

ALEX   September 3, 2008. Thursday. Okay, okay, Ruby's
right. So Melody, what are you going to do now?

MELODY   I'm going to school! It's 9:05.

ALEX & RUBY   Umm, I think we'll join you.

        (RUBY, ALEX, and MELODY rush to school and RUBY spills
her hot cocoa again.)

Maria McCarthy

"THE COFFEE SHOP BRAWL"

(Before school in a crowded coffee shop. <u>RUBY</u> and <u>ALEX</u> are standing together, drinking and talking.)

<u>RUBY</u>   What do you think we're going to be learning at school today?

<u>ALEX</u>   I don't know. Maybe we're going to learn about technology.

<u>RUBY</u>   Yes, maybe we're going to learn about that.

(<u>MELODY</u> is running to school as fast as she can when she runs into <u>ALEX</u> and <u>RUBY</u>.)

(CRASH!!!! <u>ALEX</u> starts arguing with <u>MELODY</u>.)

<u>ALEX</u>   Melody, look what you've done! YOU SPILLED MY DRINK!

<u>MELODY</u>   You were in my way.

<u>ALEX</u>   Look at my clothes! This dress was new!

<u>MELODY</u>   Well, I don't care. You were in my way.

<u>ALEX</u>   Well, if you hadn't run this way, none of this would have happened.

<u>RUBY</u>   Wait, wait. What is going on here?

<u>MELODY</u>   Well, Alex was standing in my way.

<u>ALEX</u>   Well, if she had run that way instead of this way...

RUBY   Alex, I will buy you another hot tea if you
stop arguing with Melody.

ALEX   If she apologizes for spilling my drink then I
will let you buy me a new drink.

MELODY   I will not apologize.

RUBY   Well, if you just drop it then we can clean up
this mess and get out of here.

ALEX & MELODY   (at the same time) NO! We won't drop it!

RUBY   Hey, Alex and Melody! Everyone is staring at
you guys fighting.

        (ALEX and MELODY's skin color gets red and they look
around!)

ALEX & MELODY   Oops!

                (quietly, to each other) Sorry.

                (yelling, to the staring crowd) Sorry everyone!

        (They turn to RUBY and she looks happy.)

RUBY   I am happy that you stopped arguing finally.
Maybe in the future you won't fight in public.

Jasmine Sun

"LATE FOR SCHOOL"

(A small town, the present. ALEX and RUBY are talking in a coffee shop. A girl named MELODY is also there.)

MELODY   Oh no! I am late for school. I had better leave now.

(MELODY rushes by the two girls and spills ALEX's drink.)

ALEX   Hey! Look what you did to my shirt!

MELODY   Sorry, but I have to go or I'll be late for school.

ALEX   You're not going anywhere until you pay for this.

MELODY   I left my money at home.

ALEX   Go get it, then.

(MELODY checks her watch.)

MELODY   I can't. I'll be late for school. I'm already late and my mom will bust me if I'm any later.

RUBY   Alex. C'mon, let's just get another drink. It's not a big deal.

ALEX   It is too! My mom is gonna be so mad at me.

MELODY   I'm not gonna pay. I just bumped you. You're the one who spilled the drink.

ALEX   You are too paying. Go run home, and get
the money.

MELODY   Oh, fine.

          (to herself) I'll just run to school. She
wouldn't even know.

          (out loud) Bye. I'll see you soon. Maybe.

     (MELODY rushes off.)

ALEX   She seemed almost happy to leave. I have a
feeling she's got something up her sleeve.

RUBY   Alex, you've got to calm down. Why don't we
just get some more hot chocolate?

ALEX   No! I will not leave it alone! I won't tolerate
it! How come nobody understands that I am a human and I have
feelings too!

MELODY   Well, at least I've gotten away from Alex.

     (ALEX calms down temporarily.)

ALEX   Hey, Ruby, do you know what school Melody
goes to?

RUBY   Yeah. She goes to Sunrise Elementary. Why?

ALEX   I was just wondering.

RUBY   Well, I'm just gonna get my hot chocolate and
leave. My mom has to take me to my violin lesson.

     (RUBY leaves.)

ALEX   Uurgh! How come nobody ever listens to me!

     (ALEX leaves for home, and gets her bike to try to find
Sunrise Elementary.)

ALEX   I'll find that school on the net and then I'll
tell her.

        (ALEX searches. She discovers that there is no Sunrise
Elementary.)

ALEX   Waaaaahh!!! There is no Sunrise Elementary. RUBY!

        (ALEX rides her bike to RUBY's house.)

ALEX   Hello? Is anybody there? Hey! There's a note on
the door. Ruby is at her violin lesson. How fortunate.

        (An engine roars, and then shuts down.)

ALEX   Ruby! I would like you to know that there is no
Sunrise Elementary in Seattle!

RUBY   What'dya mean? I didn't say there was a Sunrise
Elementary. I said I didn't know, but my cousin Melody goes to
Sunrise Elementary in New York!

        (Later, ALEX, RUBY and MELODY see each other at the
café again.)

MELODY   I had this strange dream that I spilled a drink
on Alex's shirt.

RUBY   That's funny. I had the exact same dream.

MELODY   It seemed so real.

ALEX   Duh. It was real.

RUBY   Don't you think that's weird, Alex?

ALEX   Kinda.

        (to herself) That was so a lie. But seeing as
they aren't going to believe me, I'd better pretend this never
happened. Wait -- did this happen? Or was it really a dream?
Let's pretend it was a dream, that would be easier.

RUBY   Um, Alex? You seem like you went off and started daydreaming.

ALEX   Oh. Um. Sorry. That was kind of weird.

MELODY   Uh, Alex? I think something's bothering you.

RUBY   Yeah. Could you please tell us?

MELODY   I mean, like, we're your friends. You can trust us.

ALEX   I don't feel like talking about it.

                (to herself) Was it seriously a dream? Alex, you need to get real. Come back to the present world. Remember, there's no unscrambling scrambled eggs.

MELODY   Alex! What the heck is wrong with you?!

RUBY   Whoa, Melody. Leave her alone for a while. It's like soda. Let it sit, and it'll lose its fizziness.

        (RUBY and MELODY leave together.)

ALEX   I needed that. Now I have proven to myself that it was only a dream. Phew. Melody! Ruby! I calmed down! I lost my "fizziness" or whatever you call it. Melody? Ruby? Where are you guys?

        (ALEX looks at her watch.)

ALEX   Oh no! It's just like in the dream. I'm late for school! It's already 9:23! Mrs. Wobker is not going to like this.

Eli Mrozek

"THE SNEAK"

(GERRET, STEVEN, and REN walk on together in front of their school in Ontario, Canada.)

GERRET   See ya!

(GERRET exits the stage.)

STEVEN   (Whispers to himself.) I'm sick of him.

REN   Bye, Gerret!

(STEVEN is thoughtful. STEVEN and REN start to walk offstage. STEVEN pauses stage right.)

STEVEN   I'll make them hate each other.

(REN starts to walk offstage.)

STEVEN   Gerret says he hates you.

REN   (shocked, hurt) Tell him I hate him.

(REN exits as GERRET enters. STEVEN walks up to GERRET.)

STEVEN   Ren says he hates you.

GERRET   I'll talk to him tomorrow.

STEVEN   My plan is working!

(The next day. The boys enter.)

GERRET   Ren, you're such an idiot!

REN   No, you're the idiot!

GERRET   You jerk!

REN   Be quiet.

GERRET   You better stay away from me from now on, or else.

REN   You know, that's a good idea. I will.

GERRET   Good.

          (GERRET and REN exit.)

STEVEN   Now to end my plan!

          (The next day. REN and STEVEN enter.)

REN   I'm really sick of Gerret. He's such a jerk.

STEVEN   I know. Isn't he?

REN   Yeah he is.

STEVEN   He never really liked you.

REN   And I thought he was my friend!

STEVEN   We were completely tricked.

REN   He's terrible.

STEVEN   Well, we should really stay away from him.

REN   Well, I'm sick of him.

STEVEN   You can make new friends.

REN   Good idea. Thanks Steven!

          (REN runs offstage.)

STEVEN   Bye! (To himself.) My plan worked.

Ya Xin Huang
Jing Yi Zhen

"GIRL STOLE MONEY"

(It's a sunny morning at Mercer Middle School. LILY,
BAILEY and ZANDRA are friends. BAILEY stops to open her locker
while the other two wait. LILY watches BAILEY intently. Then
the girls head off for class. Later, when everyone else is
outside, LILY returns. She looks around, obviously making sure
no one is watching her. She successfully opens BAILEY's locker
and takes her wallet. She is not aware that ZANDRA and BAILEY
happen to see her from outside.)

BAILEY   (outraged) I'm going to tell a teacher about
this. Lily just stole my money from my locker! Some friend!

(ZANDRA gently pulls BAILEY into a corner.)

ZANDRA   Please, Bailey, don't tell the teacher that
Lily stole your money.

BAILEY   But it's my money! I was given that money from
my parents!

ZANDRA   Please, Bailey. Lily is my best friend.

BAILEY   Well, I'm your best friend, too!

ZANDRA   But you have lots of friends. Lily only has one
friend and that's me.

BAILEY   Fine - we are breaking up right now! You will
never be my friend again!

ZANDRA   Fine! You'll never be my friend again, either!

(BAILEY and ZANDRA stalk off in opposite directions,
fuming. A little time passes. LILY is looking through BAILEY's
wallet. At first, she looks happy. Then, she sits down and
sighs sadly. She is slumped over the wallet in her lap, her
head in her hands. Dejected, ZANDRA quietly sits down next to
her. She slumps over in the same pose.)

ZANDRA   Bailey and I aren't friends anymore.

LILY   (bigger sigh) I know. It's because of what I
did. It's my fault you guys aren't friends now. I thought the
money would make me happy. But now I just feel sad and afraid.

ZANDRA   Well, you probably should! Bailey wants to tell
the teacher!

LILY   Maybe I should just tell on myself. At least
that would be the truth. And I won't have to be afraid of
Bailey telling.

ZANDRA   I don't know what to tell you. I just can't
believe what you did.

LILY   (standing up) There's the teacher. I'm going to
tell her that I stole from Bailey.

     (LILY strides out leaving, ZANDRA staring after her.
Soon, she returns, obviously relieved.)

ZANDRA   Telling the truth feels better, huh?

LILY   Yeah, but there's more.

ZANDRA   Yeah! Bailey and I aren't friends now.

     (LILY hangs her head.)

LILY   That's what I mean. I stole Bailey's money
because I wanted you to break up.

ZANDRA   Well, maybe you need to...

LILY & ZANDRA   ... tell Bailey the truth!

(BAILEY walks by, checking the contents of her wallet. She is irritated to hear herself talked about, especially by the other two. She confronts them with her hands on her hips, ready to fight.)

BAILEY   What's that you're saying about me?

(ZANDRA gives LILY a look.)

LILY   Bailey, I gotta tell you the truth. That's what we were talking about. And the truth is, I stole your money because I wanted you and Zandra to break up. I thought it would make me happy. But it sure didn't.

BAILEY   (sitting down) So you went and told on yourself?

LILY   Yup. It helped some. But Zandra's my friend and she got hurt. She still wants to be friends with you, too.

ZANDRA   But not if you told on my friend Lily.

BAILEY   The teacher gave me back my wallet before I could say anything. But I was still sad.

LILY   Friends are important, huh?

BAILEY   More important than money.

ZANDRA   That's what I was trying to tell you, Bailey. Now, can we all three be friends?

BAILEY & LILY   Friends forever!

Gabriel Estrella

"FRIENDS"

MOM   Wake up! You're gonna be late!

        (JAKE looks at the alarm clock. It is 5:37 a.m.)

JAKE   It's 5:37! I need more sleep.

        (JAKE goes back to sleep. When he wakes up, it is 6:45.
JAKE runs to the bathroom, brushes his teeth, washes his face
and puts on his clothes. He runs outside to the bus stop. He just
barely catches the bus. JAKE looks around for a place to sit and
sees his friend TONY in the back, talking with friends. JAKE
goes to sit with them, but TONY's friends don't want JAKE to sit
there. JAKE goes back to the front of the bus with the nerds.)

TONY   Why don't you want Jake to sit with us?

NOAH   Because he's a nerd. Why are you even hanging
out with him?

TONY   Because he's my best friend. Why do you think
he's a nerd?

NOAH   Because he looks like a nerd.

TONY   What's wrong with being a nerd? They're smart
and there's nothing wrong with being smart.

NOAH   Nerds don't know about being cool!

TONY   What's "being cool" mean?

NOAH   It means the opposite of a nerd.

TONY   Whatever. That doesn't even make sense. And who
says that you're cool, anyway? You think you are, but you just
wait. Friendships are more important than being cool. I'm going
to sit with Jake.

        (TONY goes to sit with JAKE. At school, TONY and JAKE
walk together.)

JAKE   Are you sure you don't want to hang with those
people from the bus?

TONY   Yes, I'm sure. I prefer friends like you, who
aren't afraid of others.

        (Bell rings. TONY and JAKE go to class.)

Hamziye Ahmed

"I LOST MY FAMILY AT THE MOVIES"

(ZAMZAME, SORRY and LOLE are at the movie theater.)

ZAMZAME   Why didn't you see the movie, "I Lost My Family?"

SORRY   I didn't want to see that movie because it's
very scary!

ZAMZAME   Are you a baby?

SORRY   Come on. Be fair. That movie is horrible. I
heard that there's lots of violence, and I don't like violence!
I get nightmares. I cry. You can't force me to watch the movie.

LOLE   Zamzame, you shouldn't push Sorry to watch the
movie.

ZAMZAME   I didn't push her towards the movie! I only
asked her why she didn't watch it.

LOLE   Okay! Stop fighting. I don't like it when
friends fight.

(SORRY and ZAMZAME tell LOLE why they are fighting.)

LOLE   Okay, Sorry doesn't want to watch the movie.

(LOLE turns to speak to ZAMZAME.)

Sorry doesn't have to watch the movie if she doesn't
like it… You don't have to say, "Are you a baby?" to Sorry.
Okay, Zamzame? Don't fight anymore. You are friends and I don't
like it when friends fight!

ZAMZAME   I am sorry, Sorry.

SORRY   I am sorry, too, Zamzame.

SORRY & ZAMZAME (speaking to LOLE) We are friends!

Anna Yu

"THE PARTY"

(LONA and LILY go over to their friend JENNIFER's house for JENNIFER's birthday party. JENNIFER is 23. JENNIFER's home is large, and there is beer and cake.)

LONA   Lily, how are you doing?

LILY   Everything is okay.

JENNIFER   Hi everyone!

LONA   Lily, what did you bring to Jennifer's party?

LILY   I brought something special, a bracelet with our names on it.

JENNIFER & LONA We love it!

(LILY, JENNIFER, and LONA talk. LILY pushes LONA and spills beer on her clothes.)

LONA   Why did you push me and spill beer on my
clothes?

LILY   Because there are too many people.

JENNIFER   What happened?

LONA   Lily spilled beer on my clothes.

LILY   Sorry.

JENNIFER   Why did you do that, Lily?

LILY   (worried) Because she told you that I am
a bad girl!

JENNIFER   Lona didn't tell me that you are a bad girl.

LILY   You are lying!

LONA   No, she is not.

JENNIFER   Lily, say you're sorry to Lona.

LILY   I'm sorry, Lona.

LONA   It's okay. I made a mistake. It's no one's fault.

        (JENNIFER, LILY and LONA are best friends again.)

Jazmin Moreno
Katy Lei

"APOLOGY"

(Brothers <u>JAKE</u> and <u>MICHAEL</u> are at home with <u>MOM</u>.)

<u>MOM</u>   Hey, Jake! Can you go to the supermarket with your brother to get some cheese, milk and chicken for dinner, please?

<u>JAKE</u>   Okay, Mom! Hey, Michael! Stop watching TV and come with me to the supermarket.

<u>MICHAEL</u>   Okay, just one second. Let me close the TV and put on my shoes.

<u>MOM</u>   All right boys, don't forget, sharp cheddar cheese, a gallon of low-fat milk and a roasted chicken.

<u>MICHAEL</u> & <u>JAKE</u>   Okay!

(They are walking to the store.)

<u>MICHAEL</u>   Three blocks to go, right?

<u>JAKE</u>   Yeah, how did you know?

<u>MICHAEL</u>   Mom showed me yesterday.

<u>JAKE</u>   Oh, good! I guess I can go home now, because you know how to get there. Here's the money! Bye.

<u>MICHAEL</u>   What are you doing? How am I suppose to carry everything that Mom wanted? I'm only eight years old! It'll all be too heavy for me.

<u>JAKE</u>   All right, just calm down. I was just joking.

MICHAEL   Well, I don't like your stupid jokes. They are
not funny.

JAKE   Okay, whatever, I don't care. Hey, aren't those
my classmates?

MICHAEL   Those guys at the park?

JAKE   I am not talking to you.

MICHAEL   Then who are you talking to?

JAKE   Myself! Yeah, those are my classmates. Hey guys!
What are you doing here?

CLASSMATES   Hey, how are you doing? We're playing
basketball. What are you doing here?

JAKE   My mom asked me to go to the supermarket
with him.

          (JAKE points at MICHAEL.)

CLASSMATES   Oh! Hah!

          (CLASSMATES all laugh.)

JAKE   Hey, do you want to hear something funny? Well,
you know what Michael told me last night?

CLASSMATES   What? What was so funny?

JAKE   He told me that he had a really scary dream...
about a pink monster with big clown shoes as ears!

CLASSMATES   What a baby!

          (They all laugh more. MICHAEL runs away.)

JAKE   Michael! Got to go, he is probably gonna go
cry to Mom.

CLASSMATES   All right, see you tomorrow at school.

JAKE   Yeah, good thing that Mom taught him how to get home from here, so I don't have to worry too much. Bye!

(JAKE finds MICHAEL at home.)

MICHAEL   Mom, Jake was bothering me all the way to the supermarket.

MOM   Jake, apologize to your brother.

JAKE   Sorry, Michael.

(Two weeks later, at school.)

CLASSMATE   Kick your butt? Sure!

(JAKE's classmates kicked him for ten minutes until he realized that he had a piece of paper stuck to his back reading, "Kick me.")

(JAKE returns home after a really embarrassing day at school.)

JAKE   What did you do that for?

MICHAEL   What? What did I do?

JAKE   The paper you stuck on my back. Did you think I wouldn't know that it was you? I wasn't born yesterday.

MICHAEL   Oh, that. Well, I did it for the same reason you did what you did two weeks ago.

JAKE   It's not my fault that you won't accept my apology.

MICHAEL   Right, but it is your fault that I can't even go out in the street without someone making fun of me because of that stupid story you made up. I don't even want to go to school anymore. Don't tell me that's not your fault!

JAKE   Whatever!

   (JAKE is talking to himself.)

JAKE   I have to take a risk for my brother. He's right, all of this is my fault. I got to think of something like... hmm. I know! I'll do exactly what I did to Michael, but this time, I'll make fun of myself in front of my classmates.

JAKE   Hey, Mom, can I take Michael to school today?

MOM   Sure, what for?

JAKE   Well, I want to show him something.

   (MICHAEL comes down the stairs.)

MOM   Hey Michael, Jake will take you to school today.

MICHAEL   Why aren't you taking me?

MOM   Because your brother wants to.

MICHAEL   Okay, Mom.

JAKE   Let's go.

MICHAEL   Why are you taking me to school today?

JAKE   'Cause I want to show you something.

MICHAEL   Hey, where are you going? That isn't the way to my school.

JAKE   Yeah, about that, we are not going to your school. We are going to my school first.

MICHAEL   Why?

JAKE   I told you, I want to show you something. And here we are.

CLASSMATES   Hey Jake, why did you bring your little brother here?

JAKE   I want to tell you guys something... I... I...

CLASSMATES   What are you going to tell us? Are you going to tell us another one of your brother's stupid dreams?

JAKE   No!

(MICHAEL runs away.)

JAKE   Where are you going?

CLASSMATES   Just let him go, he is probably going to cry to your mom like a little baby.

JAKE   Man, I gotta find him. If he tells Mom, she'll ground me!

(MICHAEL is hiding a few feet away and hears what JAKE said. He comes out.)

MICHAEL   You see? You're always thinking about yourself. You only care that Mom might ground you, but what if I get lost? You probably wouldn't care, right, because you don't ask yourself how I feel!

JAKE   You're right, I don't ask how you feel. But when you told me that you couldn't even go out onto the streets without someone making fun of you, I decided to embarrass myself in front of my classmates so we could be even. And then maybe you would accept my apology, but apparently, everything went wrong. And I am sorry that I made up that story about your dream. I wish you would forgive me.

MICHAEL   Can you just take me home?

JAKE   (sighs) Okay, let's go.

MICHAEL   Mom, can you drive us to school?

MOM   Why are you here? Wasn't Jake supposed to take
you to school?

JAKE   It's a long story, tell you later.

MICHAEL   Yeah, and... take Jake first, I don't want him
to be late to school.

          (They get into the car.)

MICHAEL   I can help you get even.

JAKE   What do you mean?

MICHAEL   Oh, you'll see.

MOM   Okay! We are here, Jake.

JAKE   Thanks Mom! Bye.

          (JAKE gets out of the car and goes into school.)

MOM   Okay, let's go to your school, Michael.

MICHAEL   Oh, no, wait! I have to do something here.

MOM   What?

MICHAEL   I'll tell you the story really fast, because
I have to get to Jake's class before he gets there. He'll take
his time, so I have a minute. You see, we had a fight because
he embarrassed me in front of his friends and now everybody
makes fun of me. That was why I didn't talk to him for two
weeks. And today, when he said he was going to bring me to
school, he brought me here instead and then tried to make fun
of himself in front of his friends so that we would be even.
But his classmates started laughing at me, so I ran away, and
now I've told him that I could help him get even. So that's
what I am going to do now. So can you wait here? Please?

MOM   Wow, that was a very long story, but you are
not going up there alone.

MICHAEL   Please trust me! Look, if I don't come back
in five minutes, just go up to Room 108 and look for me. But
please let me do it.

MOM   Okay, I guess you guys are old enough to solve
your problems.

MICHAEL   So is that a yes?

MOM   Yes, but only five minutes, okay?

MICHAEL   Thanks Mom. And oh, please don't punish Jake.
He'll learn his lesson now.

MOM   Okay. I wonder what you are going to do to him.

          (MICHAEL gets to the classroom, JAKE is not there yet and
the teacher had gone to take the attendance sheet to the office.
MICHAEL writes "Jake loves Jessica" on the board. JAKE's classmates start to point and laugh. JAKE walks into the classroom.)

JAKE   What the... Jake loves Jessica? No I don't.

CLASSMATES   Jake likes the ugly girl! Hah!

JAKE   Michael! What are you doing here?

MICHAEL   I told Mom everything, and she let me come
here and do this. She said we are old enough to solve our own
problems. Oh, and don't worry, she promised that she wouldn't
punish you.

JAKE   Where are you going?

MICHAEL   I told Mom that I'd be back in five minutes. I
got to go.

JAKE   But what am I going to do? My classmates are
going to laugh at me all day long.

MICHAEL   Deal with it.

(After school...)

JAKE   So that is what I get for being so mean.

MICHAEL   Yeah, you deserved it.

JAKE   Don't push it.

MICHAEL   I was just joking.

JAKE   So now that we are even, can you accept my
apology?

MICHAEL   Yeah, but don't do that ever again!

JAKE   Okay!

Tiffiny Pham

"LOVE AND LIES"

(JENNY and CINDY are hanging out backstage with DAVID, CINDY's boyfriend, who is a famous rock star. DAVID is doing his hair after his concert. They are getting ready to go to the after-party.)

JENNY   David, I think I gotta tell you the truth.

DAVID   What? What truth? (pause) I think maybe we should talk later because I'm very busy right now, okay?

CINDY   Is this important?

JENNY   Yes and I gotta tell you right now. David, I love you!

DAVID & CINDY   What?

DAVID   What? What did you just say? You love me? Hahahahahaha... Uh, I know, and I love you, too!

CINDY   You're kidding, right?

JENNY   No! I know this sounds crazy and I told myself that I have to stop thinking about you, but I can't. You're always on my mind. When I see you and Cindy having fun together, I feel so jealous. I don't know how I could have that feeling, and I don't even know when I fell in love with you. I didn't know what to do, but I knew I needed to tell you. I really love you, David!

DAVID   (brushing his hair) Wow. Uh, this so crazy. What the heck are you talking about?

CINDY   Are you OK, Jenny? I don't think you know what you're talking about.

JENNY   Cindy, you're a very good friend, and I'm sorry
but I know exactly what I'm talking about. David, I really love
you and I just wanted to tell you about my feelings. We have
known each other for a long time, and Cindy showed up just when
I wanted to tell you about my feelings!

CINDY   What? But you're the one who introduced me to
David. Remember?

JENNY   You still don't understand? I gave up my love
for you.

CINDY   What? Did I hear correctly? You gave up David
for me? Oh my gosh, what's going on here?

JENNY   I felt sorry for you, but now I feel sorry for
me. And soon I will lose my love forever, because you guys are
going to get married this month. Now I feel like I'm so stupid!

CINDY   And you're trying to stop my wedding?

JENNY   No, I just wanted to tell him my feelings.

DAVID   So, now what?

JENNY   David, I really love you and now you know '
that. I don't know what's going to happen next, but I feel much
better because I could shift that burden off my shoulders. And
I have to tell you one more important thing. You will thank me
after you hear this!

          (JENNY turns to CINDY.)

JENNY   My best friend, I would never have told David
about my feelings if I didn't know about your secret.

CINDY   What secret?

JENNY   David, listen. Did someone tell you that your
pretty girlfriend has been in bed with another guy while you
two were a couple?

DAVID   What? What did you just say? Cindy, is that true?

CINDY   How could you believe her? She is jealous and
trying to take you away from me!

JENNY   Well, I confess that I am jealous, but I'm not
lying. David, just take a look at these pictures and then you
will understand.

          (DAVID looks at the pictures. He turns and looks at
CINDY for a long time. CINDY suddenly hugs him.)

CINDY   I'm sorry. That day, I...

DAVID   I don't want to hear any excuses! How could you?

JENNY   Tell me, David, have you ever loved me?

DAVID   Jenny, thanks a lot for telling me that secret.
I want you to know that you're a good friend. I like you a lot.
But I just like you as a friend. I'm so sorry.

          (JENNY cries and runs away. CINDY and DAVID are left in
the room crying.)

DAVID   Cindy, my love for you was so true, and my
heart was telling me that you loved me, too! But now...

CINDY   Please, I'm sorry and I love you too, I do...

DAVID   How can I trust you any more?

CINDY   Da... vid.

DAVID   Don't ever call me again. I don't want to see
you anymore. And if in the future, we accidentally see each
other, please pretend that we don't know each other. Bye!

          (DAVID runs away, leaving CINDY alone in the room
crying. After a moment, DAVID walks slowly back on stage behind
CINDY and hugs her.)

Lili Ann Alvarado

"NENA'S DILEMMA"

(NENA and SHELBY are in fifth period gym class.)

NENA   (sighs) Shelby, I can't stop thinking of
Javier. He's so bomb.

SHELBY   Well, if you really like him, then you should
ask him out. Or at least talk to him.

NENA   Yeah, I guess you're right.

(The bell rings, and fifth period ends.)

SHELBY   So what's your next period?

NENA   Ms. Lu, Math Improvement, and it's not a class
for mental people so don't even think about saying that.

SHELBY   Yeah, whatever.

NENA   (to herself) Why doesn't Javier notice me? I
wonder if Javier will be in class today? I think I'm going to
talk to Beto. He's friends with Javier. Maybe I can find out if
Javier wants to get to know me. Maybe at the dance?

NENA   Oh, Beto. I was just thinking about you. I have
a problem. Can you help me?

BETO   Cool, sure, I can solve anything. I am here to
help. Uh, can't talk now. See you. Let's talk during break!

NENA   Beto, come back here. I need you now! Where are
you going? Okay, during break.

(It's break, and students are pouring out of class in a constant stream, like someone just took the top off of a bottle. NENA stands in the hall, looking for BETO and catches JAVIER's eye.)

JAVIER   What's the matter with you?

NENA   Oh Javier! Oh, nothing. I'm just looking for someone. What are you doing?

JAVIER   Nena, you look lost. I hope you find whoever you're looking for. Catch you later.

NENA   Sure thing. Oh! Beto. Where have you been? Why are you never here when I need you?

BETO   What's up with you? You look totally mental. What's going on?

NENA   Please don't tell anybody! Okay, I was just wondering if Javier would ever talk to me. You know him, right?

BETO   Why do you want to talk to that spikey haired dude? Yeah, I know him. What do you want to talk to him about?

(NENA looks upset and flustered. She stares ahead and then shrugs her shoulders.)

NENA   I want to get to know him. Will he be at the dance? Do you know?

(BETO bursts out laughing.)

BETO   You like him! You are crazy! Okay, I'll talk to him. I'll tell him you are in love with him!

NENA   Noooo. Just tell him that I'll see him at the dance.

BETO   I'm cool.

NENA   Thanks, Beto.

        (BETO walks over to his friends.)

BETO   (loudly) Do you want to know what Nena just told me?

NENA   (shouting) Stop!

BETO   Just joking. Ha, ha!

        (At the dance, NENA is dancing with her friends and sees JAVIER looking her way. JAVIER walks slowly towards her.)

JAVIER   What's up?

NENA   Not much. What about you?

        (They walk off together.)

Brenda Morales

"FIGHTING FOR A GIRL"

(LISSETH, walking while not looking, bumps into two boys, JOSE and LUIS, who are walking and talking. They both see that she is one hot chick.)

JOSE & LUIS   Wow! Sorry!

(They walk away.)

JOSE   Damn, she is fine.

LUIS   I know. I'm gonna ask her out.

JOSE   I was going to do that!

LUIS   I don't care.

JOSE   Well I do, so back off.

LUIS   No.

JOSE   Okay, we both ask her out, and let's see who she says yes to, okay?

LUIS   Okay, but when?

JOSE   After school. 2:30 p.m.

LUIS   Okay, fine.

JOSE   Watch me win!

LUIS   I'm gonna win!

116.

JOSE   Shut up, okay?

LUIS   Shut up!

JOSE   You!

        (The bell rings. They both are late for class. The
principal is in the hallway. They both run out.)

        (The bell rings again. School is over. LUIS and JOSE
run to LISSETH.)

LUIS & JOSE   Do you want to go out with me?

LISSETH   Umm, first, I have to see how well you get
along with my parents.

LUIS & JOSE   Oh.

LISSETH   Then I wanna see if either of you guys is
my type.

JOSE   That would be me.

LUIS   No it won't, it will be me. Why would she
pick you?

JOSE   It will be me, because I'm sexy and you're not.

        (He pushes LUIS.)

LISSETH   Stop fighting, OK?

JOSE & LUIS   Sorry!

LISSETH   Whateva! After that, you guys have to fight
each other tomorrow.

JOSE   Okay, I'm down with it. I'm gonna beat him
tomorrow.

LUIS   No, I'm gonna beat you.

JOSE   No, you're not.

LISSETH   You guys! Tomorrow, you guys can fight.

JOSE   No, we should fight right now.

LUIS   Okay, let's go.

JOSE   Fine.

        (They drop their stuff on the floor and they both take
off their shirts.)

LISSETH   Stop, or I won't go out with either of you guys!

        (They both stop, but they're really angry. They both
give LISSETH a hug as they leave.)

LISSETH   Um, bye.

        (The next day, end of school. LUIS is waiting and
waiting in the park and JOSE doesn't show up. But JOSE is
hiding. JOSE runs up to LUIS and starts beating him up.)

LUIS   What the heck is your problem?

JOSE   I told you I was gonna beat you up!

LUIS   Shut up!

        (JOSE punches him in the eye and stomach, then LUIS
punches him back and then all of the sudden LISSETH comes
running and watches them fight. Two minutes later, JOSE knocks
LUIS down.)

JOSE   Hahaha! I won!

LUIS   Shut up.

JOSE   Say whatever you want. At least I got Lisseth
to go out with me.

LISSETH   Let's go, Jose.

JOSE   Okay, let's go.

      (Two weeks later in the hall at school, JOSE and LUIS
are both walking in the halls with a girl next to them.)

JOSE   What's up? You still mad at me?

LUIS   Nope, it's okay.

JOSE   Oh, okay.

LUIS   Hey, this is my girlfriend. Her name is Joselyn.

JOSE   Oh, nice to meet you.

JOSE   Hey, all four of us should go to the movies
tomorrow.

LUIS   Good idea. Okay, then, see you guys later.

JOSE   Bye.

LISSETH   Bye.

Lina Maki
Mitzy Torres Brown

"DENZEL IS ALL MINE"

(SHELBY and NATALIE meet by the fountain at Lynwood Mall to buy some clothes for the Halloween dance at school.)

SHELBY   The dance is only two days away!

NATALIE   Yeah, I know. I saw this pretty hot costume...

SHELBY   There's that really cute guy named Denzel!

NATALIE   Oh, Denzel. You like him?

          (She plays with her hair.)

SHELBY   He's really cute! You know him?

NATALIE   Yeah, I see him around school.

SHELBY   OMG! Look, he's right there!

          (SHELBY and NATALIE both say hi nervously.)

DENZEL   (to SHELBY) Don't I know you?

SHELBY   Yeah, uh, you're in my math class, fifth period.

NATALIE   Hi, I'm Natalie.

DENZEL   Yeah, uh, I've seen you around school.

SHELBY   You want to hang out with us?

DENZEL   Sure, sounds great.

NATALIE   I'm kind of hungry. You want to get something to eat?

(DENZEL and SHELBY agree.)

NATALIE   Let's get some pizza!

(They walk over to the food court. DENZEL is three steps in front of them. Both girls whisper about having a crush on him.)

SHELBY   You look like you like him too!

NATALIE   Okay. So I like him too. So what? He looks lonely. Let's go!

(NATALIE walks away as SHELBY follows. SHELBY offers to buy DENZEL a pizza. NATALIE gets mad and asks him if he wants to share a drink.)

DENZEL   Yeah, but I want a different straw, please.

NATALIE   (in a low voice) Yeah, sure.

(They all finish their pizza and drinks.)

DENZEL   Oh, I'm waiting for someone.

SHELBY & NATALIE Who?

DENZEL   (proudly) My girlfriend.

(Both girls are shocked to find out that DENZEL already has a girl.)

Melina Nguyen-Reyes
Jordyn Jarvis

"LOVE IS COMPLICATED"

(At the coffee shop.)

ISABELLA   Hey babe! What are we planning to do for
graduation?

CHRIS   Um... well... I don't know... because... well...

ISABELLA   I was thinking, maybe we could go to dinner or
maybe have a party or...

CHRIS   I don't think any of that will work out.

ISABELLA   Then what the heck are we going to do?

CHRIS   (annoyed) Nothing!

ISABELLA   What's that suppose to mean?

CHRIS   I don't know how to say this.

(CHRIS takes a sip of his Frappuccino.)

ISABELLA   What do you mean? What don't you know ho--?

CHRIS   (quietly) I don't want to be with you anymore.

ISABELLA   What?

CHRIS   Don't make me say it again. It hurt the
first time.

ISABELLA   (quietly) Why?

CHRIS   Just ... I don't know. Just go. Just leave
me alone.

ISABELLA   Fine!

          (ISABELLA slams her coffee down on the table and storms
out. CHRIS sighs loudly.)

          (Four years later, in New York.)

ISABELLA   Oh my god, wake up hun! Today is our big day!

ANGELA   Yes! I have been waiting for this day for what
seems like forever!

ISABELLA   So I'll pick up my dress.

ANGELA   Did you choose the one with the flowers on
the straps?

ISABELLA   Um, I can't tell you! It's bad luck!

ANGELA   Okay! Love you! See you soon!

ISABELLA   Love you, too. Bye!

          (ISABELLA is picking up her dress at the boutique, when
all of a sudden, she sees CHRIS.)

ISABELLA   Chris!

CHRIS   Hey! Long time no see. Since graduation, right?

ISABELLA   Yeah.

CHRIS   What are you doing today?

ISABELLA   Getting married!

CHRIS   Oh. Wow. Who's the lucky man?

ISABELLA   Um, well, lucky woman, actually.

CHRIS   Oh! What a surprise. Not to be rude or anything.

ISABELLA   Yeah.

CHRIS   When did you realize that you were going to go
the opposite direction?

ISABELLA   Well, after we, well, you know, split.

CHRIS   Oh, I see. Where's the wedding?

ISABELLA   In the church on 155th Street and 2nd Avenue.

CHRIS   Oh really? That's a very nice place to have...
a very elegant place to get married.

ISABELLA   Yeah, I suppose so.

CHRIS   I don't recall getting invited.

ISABELLA   Oh, I'm sorry. I didn't know you still lived
around here.

CHRIS   Ha. I see, well I can't blame you for not
knowing. We weren't talking anymore.

ISABELLA   Yeah. Well, look at the time! I have to get
back to Angela! Feel free to come if you'd like! I'm sure we
have enough room for one more!

CHRIS   Oh, cool. Yeah, I'll be there.

          (The wedding is starting. The Wedding March is playing.)

ISABELLA   (quietly, to herself) What am I doing?

NARRATOR   Everything was going fine, until the priest
asked if there were any objections.

CHRIS   I object!

ANGELA   Who's that?

ISABELLA   Oh my god!

ANGELA   I assume you invited him? Who is he?

ISABELLA   He's my ex-boyfriend from high school.

ANGELA   That's Chris? Him?

CHRIS   I love you Isabella. And I really do regret leaving you. I'm really sorry!

ISABELLA   What the heck. You think you can come in here and crash my wedding like this, and say sorry for a stupid high school break up. (pause) Why did you break up with me in first place?

CHRIS   Because it was going to be hard with college and all! I thought breaking up would be easier for us!

ANGELA   Um. This isn't really the time for this argument.

ISABELLA   I'm sorry, Angela. The wedding is off!

ANGELA   What?! You put me through all this for nothing! And you're leaving me for him?

ISABELLA   Well, I'm not leaving you for him. I just have to figure out my life, and what to do with it. Again, I'm really sorry.

My Linh Nguyen
Sara Abbasian

"DECISIONS"

(Sisters MAYA and KIM are in KIM's bedroom, talking.)

KIM   (whispering) Maya, I have to tell you something.

(MAYA bends over to listen.)

MAYA   What Kim? What is it?

KIM   You know how we always get into fights with Mom about stupid little things?

MAYA   What stupid things?

KIM   Like, you know, how we can't have any friends over, and we can't be on the phone for more then ten minutes.

MAYA   I hate those rules! Do you remember when I was younger, and I spilled my soup all over my new clothes, and Mom said if I did that again I wasn't allowed to watch T.V. for a whole month?

KIM   Yeah. I remember that! I got so mad at Mom.

MAYA   Anyway, what were you saying?

(KIM gets off her bed and starts pacing around.)

KIM   Well, I'm deciding to…

MAYA   What? What are you going to do?

KIM   I'm deciding to run away, and since you're my sister, I want you to come with me.

MAYA   You can't possibly be serious?!

KIM   What? What's wrong with that?

MAYA   Do you have any idea how much trouble we would
get into?

KIM   I know, but don't you think it would be worth it?

MAYA   Of course not! Running away never solves
anything!

KIM   You know what, Maya? If you don't want to do
this with me, then I'm going solo!

MAYA   No, Kim! You can't do this!

KIM   Why not?

MAYA   Because...

KIM   (angry) Because what?

MAYA   Because if you run away, I'm going to tell Mom!

KIM   (yelling) What? I know you wouldn't do that!
You're my sister! I trust you!

MAYA   I'm sorry, Kim, but when you're going to do
something this dangerous and serious, I have no other choice.

KIM   You're not serious, are you?

MAYA   I'm serious about this, Kim!

        (KIM gets up and gets a bag from the closet and starts
packing clothes.)

KIM   Well, you know what? I'm serious about
running away!

MAYA   Kim! You can't do this!

KIM   Well I am!

> (The next day, MAYA tried to find KIM, but she couldn't find her. She knew instantly that KIM had run away. She ran down the stairs, freaking out and crying, to tell MOM.)

MAYA   Mom! Mom! Mom! You'll never believe this!

MOM   What sweetie, what is it?

MAYA   (crying) I know you may not believe me, but last night while you and I were sleeping, Kim snuck out... she ran away!

MOM   (confused) What? Why would she do such a crazy thing?

MAYA   She was talking to me the other day how you and her always get into stupid fights, and she said she was sick and tired of it.

MOM   She could've told me that, and we could've solved those problems together. Running away never solves anything!

MAYA   That's what I told her!

MOM   (concerned) What are we going to do? I'm so worried about her! She's out there alone!

MAYA   So what are we going to do?

MOM   We have to find her, of course!

MAYA   How? She could be anywhere!

MOM   We will just have to go everywhere and find her!

MAYA   That's not a bad idea.

MOM   We will have to check everywhere that she hangs out with her friends.

MAYA   Perfect!

MOM   Maya, get your stuff ready. We're going
right now.

          (A couple of hours later, MAYA and MOM are searching
for KIM.)

MAYA   Kim! Kim! Where are you?!

MOM   Sweetie! Mommy and Maya are looking for you!

MAYA   She could be anywhere by now!

MOM   Yeah, how are we going to find her now? I'm so
worried that she might get kidnapped.

MAYA   I hope she's okay.

MOM   Where else could she be?

MAYA   (not paying attention) Yes!

MOM   What are you doing? Listen! I have to ask you
a question.

MAYA   (distracted) Oh nothing! What is it, Mom?

MOM   Do you know where else she could be? You're
almost always with her.

MAYA   I'm not sure but I think I might know!

MOM   Well, don't just stand there! Tell me!

MAYA   I'm not sure. I think...

MOM   Well, a guess is better than nothing.

MAYA   Well, sometimes, Kim and her friends go to the
movie theaters to hang out with her friends after school.

MOM   (excited) What movie theater? Where?

MAYA   I'm not sure about that!

MOM   I think that we can still find her. There aren't many movie theaters in town.

MAYA   You're right! We'll go to all the movie theaters in town, and I'm sure that we can find her!

                       (MAYA and MOM went to the closest movie theater first, but unfortunately she was not there. They went to the second movie theater, but she was not there. They went to almost every movie theater in town. MAYA and MOM were exhausted. But there was one more movie theater. They marched into the last movie theater with hope. MAYA saw someone standing by the popcorn machine. It was KIM!)

MAYA & MOM   Oh my goodness! We finally found Kim!

MOM   Where have you been, young lady?

KIM   Mom! Maya! What are you doing here? You're embarrassing me in front of all my friends! Get out of here!

MOM   You're coming home with me right now!

KIM   I'm not going anywhere with you!

MOM   What are you talking about? You know how worried we were?

KIM   I don't care you! You deserve it!

MOM   How do I deserve it?

KIM   Well, sometimes I feel like you don't care about me!

MOM   How could you ever say that? Do you know how worried we were? We searched all over town for you.

KIM   You and Maya searched all over town for me?

MOM   Of course we did! Do you know how worried
we were?

KIM   Mom! I'm so sorry for what I did! I feel so
stupid! I owe you and Maya an apology.

        (KIM and MOM start crying and hugging each other.)

        (Back home, where everything is normal...)

KIM   Maya, I feel like I can't trust you anymore.

MAYA   What? Why?

KIM   After what happened. I feel like I can't trust
you anymore.

MAYA   (yelling) Are you out of your mind? Without
me telling Mom, you would still be out there! Who knows what
could've happened to you?!

KIM   You know, once I think about it, I think you
might be right.

MAYA   I knew you would understand.

KIM   (smiling) I love you, Maya!

MAYA   I love you too, Kim!

Chapter 4

Drama

Abdulwahab Hilowle

"THE NEIGHBOR PROBLEM"

(<u>ANDRES</u> waves at <u>JOHN</u> outside.)

<u>ANDRES</u>   Hi, neighbor.

<u>JOHN</u>   Welcome to the 'hood.

(<u>JOHN</u> goes into his home and sees his wife <u>JACKIE</u>.)

<u>JACKIE</u>   John, you are a lazy man. All you do is sit around, drink beer, eat chips, and watch TV. You never help me out with anything!

(<u>JOHN</u> is getting angry.)

<u>JOHN</u>   I will do this later! Leave me alone now, please.

(<u>ANDRES</u> wakes up in the morning and brushes his teeth. The fighting annoys him. He knocks on <u>JACKIE</u> and <u>JOHN</u>'s door.)

<u>ANDRES</u>   You guys have been having problems lately. I came to this neighborhood to enjoy my life, and to have good neighbors. Is there any way you guys could talk about your problems calmly? It would mean a lot to me.

<u>JOHN</u>   Okay, we'll try.

(<u>JOHN</u> and <u>ANDRES</u> meet at the store after another night of fighting.)

<u>ANDRES</u>   I talked to you about the fighting problem and you didn't solve it. I'm warning you, I may call the cops if it happens again!

(<u>ANDRES</u> and <u>CLAIRE</u> are at <u>CLAIRE</u>'s home.)

ANDRES   I want you to help me with this problem I'm having with my neighbors.

CLAIRE   What kind of a problem?

ANDRES   My neighbors are fighting and it's too loud. I tried to get them to talk it out. I've warned them many times. Nothing is helping. So will you come over and pretend we're fighting?

CLAIRE   How would that help?

ANDRES   If they hear us fighting, then maybe they will understand how I am feeling.

CLAIRE   Aha, now I understand.

          (ANDRES and CLAIRE at ANDRES' house.)

CLAIRE   When I met you, I thought we were going to be together but we can't because you are a teacher! You and I have fun just sometimes. Quit your job.

ANDRES   Quit my job? Are you crazy? Why do I have to quit my job?

CLAIRE   Because you don't have any time for me!

ANDRES   What do you mean?

CLAIRE   Like going to the movies or to the park. Just somewhere that you and I can enjoy being together!

ANDRES   You want me to quit my job so that I have more time for you?

CLAIRE   Yes!

ANDRES   So how am I supposed to pay my rent?

CLAIRE   I don't know. Try to get an easier job!

ANDRES   Are you crazy? Teaching is my life! I'm not going to quit my job.

CLAIRE   So be it. You and I are through!

ANDRES   WHAT?

CLAIRE   Yeah, you heard what I said. We are through!

ANDRES   Okay. We are through.

        (The next day in JOHN and JACKIE's apartment.)

JOHN   Honey, did you hear that? They broke up.

JACKIE   They were so good together! I don't want us to fight again and end up like that.

        (JACKIE and JOHN hold hands.)

Biciok Kiir
Rian Trinh

"ILLEGAL ENTRANCE"

(JUAN, JULIO and JOSE meet at the taco stand.)

NARRATOR   Juan is 16 years old. He is tired of living
in Guatemala and wants to go to the U.S. But he could only go
illegally.

JUAN   Hey, Julio. How's it going?

JULIO,   Fine, just came by for a taco. Oh yeah, this is
my brother, Jose.

JUAN: Oh, nice to meet you, Jose.

JOSE   Hey.

NARRATOR   Jose is kinda shy. He doesn't talk much, but
he is tired of living in Mexico. He just wants to get out of
Mexico. He doesn't really care where he goes.

        (JUAN sat down, so did JULIO and JOSE.)

JUAN   Hey Julio, I need your help.

JULIO   What are you trying to do?

JUAN   Let's leave the country and go to the U.S.

JOSE   Can I help?

JUAN   Yeah, sure, we need as much help as we can get.
Julio, are you coming?

NARRATOR   Julio isn't sure if he wants to go but he doesn't want his little brother Juan to go alone.

JULIO   I guess. So what is the plan?

JUAN   We are going to cross the border. But first, let's stop by the taco shack and grab a taco.

JULIO   What? Are you crazy?

JUAN   Are you coming or not?

JULIO   I guess, but only if Jose is going and if we get some tacos.

JOSE   I want a burrito!

JUAN   Shut up! There's no rice here!

JOSE   I don't want rice; that's for Asian people.

JULIO   Here's the plan! We'll go at midnight and sneak across the canals. Then we'll claw under the gate, one by one. Make sure no one sees you!

JUAN   What about our families?

JULIO   Don't worry about it.

JUAN   No?

JULIO   What are you worried about?

JUAN   Remember the last big plan you had? It went really badly.

Elizabeth C. West

"WHAT TO DO?"

(Phone rings, KAYLA answers the phone.)

KAYLA   Hello?

CLAIRE   Hey, it's Claire! I wanted to tell you I have a
break in school coming up soon. Very soon!

KAYLA   Great! When?

CLAIRE   December twenty-first through January second,
I think.

KAYLA   Oh, yay! I'm free too. I'm taking a break from
weddings because I don't have many people around this time of
year. I'm just teaching twice a week. How about you come out here,
and take a horseback riding lesson on my special horse, Earl.

CLAIRE   (hesitantly) Okay...

KAYLA   Okay! Bye for now, honey!

CLAIRE   Bye.

          (They both hang up.)

CLAIRE   Oh man...

MELISSA   What is it, dear?

CLAIRE   Now I have to spend forty dollars on a
riding lesson.

MELISSA   Why?

CLAIRE   Because I can't say no. Kayla asked me if I
wanted a lesson, and I want it, but it's so expensive. And I
just had to say yes, even though I can't afford it, so it's
kind of not okay with me, I guess.

MELISSA   Well, do you want the lesson?

CLAIRE   Yeah, I do. It's just that I want a cheaper
lesson. I only have sixty dollars for Christmas and I've been
saving up for a while. If I spend forty, then I'll have to get
everyone things from a dollar store. And besides, I wanted to
have some money left over.

MELISSA   Well, why don't you talk to Kayla? She might be
able to talk to Joe about a shorter and cheaper lesson.

CLAIRE   I don't know.

MELISSA   Well, think about it.

          (CLAIRE leaves the room and her mom keeps cooking. She
comes back into the room a minute later.)

CLAIRE   Hey, I have an idea. But you may not agree with
it...

MELISSA   Well, what is it, honey?

CLAIRE   I was thinking, maybe you could pay for it?

MELISSA   No.

CLAIRE   Why not? You're the richest in the household.
Come on, Mom.

MELISSA   Well, for starters, it's your lesson, and taxes
are coming up. Plus, this house runs on a budget.

CLAIRE   (whispering) Stupid budgets... (in a louder
voice) Fine if you won't pay all, then maybe half, please?

MELISSA   No! Twenty dollars is a lot, you know.

CLAIRE   Yeah, I know.

MELISSA   I'm not going to pay for any of it.

CLAIRE   Fine. Don't let me have fun.

MELISSA   Sorry.

CLAIRE   I'll just have to call later and tell her I can't make it.

        (CLAIRE leaves the room sadly.)

        (Later, dinner is ready.)

MELISSA   Claire, come down! It's time to eat.

CLAIRE   Okay, just a minute! I gotta finish this e-mail.

        (She comes downstairs.)

CLAIRE   Sorry about that. I wanted to e-mail Kayla instead of talking to her on the phone.

MELISSA   It's fine. Oh, I made your favorite, so you better eat.

CLAIRE   I know, I could smell it from upstairs. And I will eat a lot!

MELISSA   Good.

CLAIRE   You know, Kayla is family to me and you and my friends are too. It's so hard.

MELISSA   Oh. (Her mouth is full. She swallows.)

CLAIRE   Anyways, what do you want for Christmas?

MELISSA   I don't know, but to save money, you could make something handmade and it would be even more special than something store-bought. Especially for family and friends. Just a thought, because then you could still have the riding lesson and see Kayla.

CLAIRE   Yeah, okay that sounds great! I will! Thanks Mom. I'll send her an e-mail tomorrow, because now I have homework to do.

MELISSA   Are you done?

CLAIRE   Yup, I think so. I feel full.

MELISSA   Better hurry! It's almost bed time.

      (CLAIRE leaves the room. Fifteen minutes later...)

CLAIRE   I'm done. I'm going to bed now!

MELISSA   (shouts from downstairs) It's about time.

      (The phone rings.)

KAYLA   Hello.

CLAIRE   Hey.

KAYLA   Hey, is this Claire?

CLAIRE   Yup! Guess what!

KAYLA   What?

CLAIRE   I have some great news!

KAYLA   Well, what is it?

CLAIRE   See, I did a lot of thinking and I decided I'm going to make gifts for Christmas this year! It will still cost money, but not as much, so I can have the lesson after all. It will be my present from me to me!

John Chan
Ali Hassan

"THE TWO BAD BOYS"

(All of the second graders are in the Fun Forest in
Seattle Center. They have just gotten off the roller coaster.
MR. KNICKS is standing in front of the roller coaster.)

MR. KNICKS   Okay kids! Stick together and don't wander
around. Now we're going to ride the bumper cars.

ERIC   Hey, Derek! Are you hungry? You want to buy
some candy?

DEREK   That's a good idea! I'm hungry too, but I don't
have any money.

ERIC   Don't worry, I'll pay for you. Let's go.

MR. KNICKS   I can hear you guys! Don't make a bad choice,
okay? If you sneak away, I will call your mom.

        (MR. KNICKS looks away.)

ERIC   Let's sneak away, Derek.

DEREK   Let's go. He's not looking!

        (ERIC and DEREK see another group of students walk by.
They both sneak into that group of students and they walk away
from their group.)

ERIK   Yes! We did it! Now let's go find the store.

DEREK   (pointing at the tree) I think it is behind
the tree!

(ERIC and DEREK find a store.)

DEREK   Let's go to this store and buy some hamburgers.

ERIC   That's McDonald's! I want candy, not hamburgers.

DEREK   I want hamburgers!

ERIC   It's my money. If you want hamburgers, pay for
it yourself.

DEREK   Let's go to this store.

ERIC   No, not this store.

DEREK   Let's look for another store.

ERIC   Hey Derek, let's try this big store. Maybe they
have some candy.

          (DEREK and ERIC finally find the store.)

DEREK   Yeah, you are right.

ERIC   They do have candy!

          (They finally buy the candy.)

DEREK   Okay, now, let's go back.

ERIC   I am kind of lost.

DEREK   Me too.

ERIC   I think we need to go that way.

DEREK   No! It's the other way.

ERIC   Okay, you go your way, and I will go my way!

DEREK   Okay! Bye.

(DEREK and ERIC go in different directions.)

MR. KNICKS   He got lost? I told you guys not to leave.
Now let's look for Eric.

          (MR. KNICKS sees ERIC walking alone.)

MR. KNICKS   What did I say to you, Eric?

ERIC   Don't call our moms, please! We will be good
next time.

DEREK   Yeah, please help! We will be good.

MR. KNICKS   That's great, but I will still call your moms.

ERIC   I am sorry! Next time, I will be good.

          (ERIC and DEREK learn their lesson.)

Tashawna Haney
Fabienne Vigil

"MOM OR PUPPY?"

(<u>KENNY</u> is with his parents, <u>SALLY</u> and <u>JOE</u>.)

<u>KENNY</u>   Good morning, mama.

<u>SALLY</u>   Honey, isn't it such a nice day today? Did you meet the new neighbors yet?

<u>KENNY</u>   No. Are they nice?

<u>JOE</u>   EWW! What's that smell?

<u>SALLY</u>   Pancakes.

<u>JOE</u>   I HATE PANCAKES, AND YOU KNOW THAT!!

<u>SALLY</u>   No I didn't. And you either eat them or you don't get anything else. Because I'm not making anything else. I have to go to work!

<u>JOE</u>   And who cares?

<u>SALLY</u>   I do. I'm not getting fired.

<u>KENNY</u>   Can I have a puppy, mama?

<u>SALLY</u>   No, you can't.

<u>JOE</u>   Yeah, you can. What's wrong wit' you, lady!

<u>SALLY</u>   Why do you want to have a puppy?

<u>KENNY</u>   'Cause I'm lonely. I have nobody to play with. None of the neighbors have kids.

SALLY   Okay, who's going to pick up the poop and take it out when you go to school?!

JOE   You!

SALLY   No, I have to work, and you always are lazy and sit on your butt and do nothing! You can do it.

    (JOE's face turns angry and he punches SALLY really hard!)

KENNY   Stop, daddy, stop!!

SALLY   Go to your room, please.

JOE   Oh no, what have I done, honey? I didn't mean to.

SALLY   I know, I know. But we have to call the police.

    (KENNY goes up to his room and closes the door. JOE gets scared and leaves to go to the bar while SALLY is in the kitchen calling the police.)

SALLY   Yes, my husband Joe just hit me and I need help.

    (KENNY goes to SALLY and starts to cry.)

SALLY   It's okay. The police are coming.

    (The police arrive and talk to SALLY. Some police stay and wait for JOE to arrive. JOE comes into the house all drunk and woozy with an eighteen-year-old blond girl. He sees the police and turns to the girl.)

JOE   Run! Go!

    (She runs.)

    (Suddenly an ambulance appears and someone slams the door open and takes SALLY. JOE gets in the police car and he is so sad. A policeman takes KENNY to his grandma's. His grandma gets him a puppy and they're both happy.)

Zoë White
Elijah Edwards

"THE KILLING"

    (On the street.)

NARRATOR   Jordan and Duran approach Nya. They both are going to ask her the same question: Will you go out with me? We'll see what happens.

JORDAN   Nya will you...

DURAN   Will you go out with me? I think you're really pretty and I really like you.

NYA   Um, sure. I didn't know you liked me like that. Yeah, I'll go out with you. Sorry, Jordan. I like you as a friend, but I like Duran more.

    (JORDAN shoves DURAN.)

JORDAN   What the--! I was going to ask her out!

DURAN   Too bad. I got to her first, and I guess I got lucky. Sorry.

NYA   Um. You two can work this out. I'll be back in a little while.

NARRATOR   Nya leaves and Jordan pulls a knife on Duran.

JORDAN   Don't step near me! I'll hurt you!

DURAN   And what if I do? It's not like you'll really stab me.

NARRATOR   Jordan stabs Duran and Duran falls.

JORDAN   That's what will happen. Sorry, but I already knew I'd get Nya before you.

NARRATOR   Jordan walks away as Nya comes back.

NYA   Oh my God!! Duran! Are you okay? Someone help me, please!

STRANGER   What happened? Why is he lying in the street like that?

NYA   He's dead!

STRANGER   He's not dead. Let me check his pulse. If he were dead, he wouldn't be breathing.

NYA   Who are you? A doctor or something?

STRANGER   Dr. Taylor. Now, tell me what happened?

NARRATOR   Duran slowly gets up and grabs his side in pain.

DURAN   I was stabbed!

DR. TAYLOR   What did you get stabbed with? I need to know if it's a big emergency or not.

DURAN   A fishing knife. It was really sharp, like he had just sharpened it. I don't know how I didn't notice it in his pocket!

DR. TAYLOR   Was it rusty? Dirty from fishing? Bloody? What?

DURAN   Well, I don't know! I was busy trying to defend myself! I'm not that observant when I'm trying to save my own life.

NYA   Duran! Relax! Did Jordan stab you?

DURAN   Yes! I hate him! He tried to kill me over a girl, and we've been friends since first grade!

DR. TAYLOR   You will have to go to the emergency with me
now, just in case that knife was infected.

DURAN   I will not go to the hospital until I get
my revenge!

NYA & DR. TAYLOR What are you going to do?

DURAN   I don't know, but I'll do something. Maybe I'll
find a branch and hit him on the side of the head with it.

NYA   If you hit him, you might get caught. You don't
want that to happen.

DURAN   I'm willing to take that chance! He tried to
kill me over a girl. He deserves it!

NYA   I hope you're as lucky as Jordan, but first you
are going to the hospital.

        (An ambulance arrives and takes DURAN, with NYA right
behind him.)

Chapter 5

Sports

C.J. De La Fuente
Said Ibrahim

"THANKS COACH"

(JAMAL and HUSSEIN are talking after school.)

HUSSEIN   Hey Jamal. You wanna go to the Northgate
Community Center?

JAMAL   What are we gonna do there?

HUSSEIN   Play basketball!

          (They go to the community center and shoot hoops.)

JAMAL   Let's play one-on-one.

HUSSEIN   Okay! Let's play up to eleven.

          (While the boys are playing, they hear a basketball
dribbling at the other end of the court. It's MR. JOHNSON.)

MR. JOHNSON   Do you want to play twenty-one? My name is Ben
Johnson. I'm a basketball coach.

JAMAL   Give us a minute to rest.

HUSSEIN   I need a drink of water.

          (They begin to play.)

MR. JOHNSON   You guys play very well.

JAMAL   Thanks!

Mr. Johnson   My team needs two more players. Do you want to
join us?

JAMAL & HUSSEIN Of course! When can we start?

MR. JOHNSON   After school, right here at the community
center! Don't be late.

JAMAL & HUSSEIN Yes, coach!

     (The next day they go to practice and do drills
and start playing games. Soon, their team wins the
championship. After the last game, HUSSEIN and JAMAL
talk to MR. JOHNSON.)

JAMAL   Coach, can you train us so we can be good
enough to get into the NCAA?

MR. JOHNSON   Sure, but you need to work hard, play well and
get into a good college.

     (Two years later, JAMAL and HUSSEIN are in college at
Harvard, playing NCAA and their coach sees them playing really
hard. A few years later, JAMAL is drafted into the NBA first.
He plays point guard with the Boston Celtics. One year later,
HUSSEIN is drafted by the Cleveland Cavaliers, where he plays
center. They play each other, and after one game, after the
Celtics win, they sit on the bench and talk.)

JAMAL   Remember when we were in high school, and we
went to the community center to play basketball?

HUSSEIN   Yeah, I remember that. When we sat on the bench
talking about the NCAA. And now we're in the NBA!

JAMAL   Thanks to Mr. Johnson.

HUSSEIN   I hope he is still coaching in high school,
but he must be very old by now.

JAMAL   Let's go back to Seattle to our old high school
and see if he's still there.

     (They return to their old high school, and talk to the
principal.)

JAMAL   Is Mr. Johnson still coaching in this school?

PRINCIPAL   Yes, but he's sick today. Maybe he will be
back tomorrow.

(They return the next day and they hear dribbling
in the gym and they go in and see <u>MR. JOHNSON</u> coaching high
school kids.)

<u>MR. JOHNSON</u>   Do I know you?

<u>JAMAL</u>   You don't remember us? You helped us go into
the NCAA! And then we got drafted into the NBA!

<u>MR. JOHNSON</u>   Oh, you are Jamal and Hussein!

<u>JAMAL</u> & <u>HUSSEIN</u> Thank you for coaching us and helping us get
into the NCAA!

Um Kalsoom
Krisna Mandujano Mazariegos
Helen Fessahaie

"MY SUPER SKATING DAY"

(At a skating rink.)

ALL   Watch it!

MIA   Get off me!

JOHANA   Get off me!

SELLY   Aah! Ouch!

(They all bump into each other. SELLY falls down.
The girls sit up, recovering.)

MIA   Are you okay?

JOHANA   Did you break a leg?

SELLY   No, but I banged my elbow and it hurts!

MIA   Let me help you stand up!

JOHANA   I will help you too.

SELLY   Thanks! I feel better already.

MIA   My name is Mia. What are yours?

JOHANA   Well, my name is Johana.

SELLY   And mine is Selly.

MIA   Do you guys want to race to the end of
the rink?

JOHANA   I do! What about you, Selly?

SELLY   I do too!

ALL   Ready, set, go!

        (The girls race to the end of the rink, all finishing
at the same time and laughing.)

MIA   You guys are good skaters… better than any
friends I know.

JOHANA   Really?

SELLY   Let's go get something to eat.

        (They go to the cafeteria.)

MIA   The food is so good here.

JOHANA   I know, but I don't have any money to buy
more food. I spent it all.

SELLY   I have some. I can spot you.

JOHANA   I'd like some cotton candy and some nachos.
Also a soda!

MIA   I would like some chips, some cotton candy and
a soda as well.

SELLY   Okay, sure.

MIA   It's a good thing we bumped into one another!

JOHANA   I know! If we hadn't bumped into one another,
Selly wouldn't have bought us this delicious food. Thanks, Selly.

        (MIA and SELLY laugh, then MIA, SELLY and JOHANA leave
happily.)

Brandon Iritani
Daniel Gonzalez

"THE CAR SHOW"

(BOB and DANIEL'S house, the present.)

(BOB and DANIEL are sitting on a couch in the living room of their house. It is littered with crushed coke cans, all the furniture is torn up, and the wallpaper is peeling. DANIEL picks up the mail from under a pile of coke cans and starts to read through it.)

DANIEL   Hey, Bob, there's something in the mail for us. It looks pretty cool. Remember last year, when we won?

BOB   Won what? What is it?

(DANIEL holds out the invitation.)

DANIEL   It's an invitation for the annual Steve Brothers' Car Show.

BOB   Oh, yeah. That's the only car show that lets two brothers enter one car.

DANIEL   Yeah, that's the one! Let's enter my Lambo again.

BOB   No, we entered that last year. And it won! Let's give my '57 BelAir a chance.

DANIEL   Come on, man! My Lambo has a lot of new features. It cost me a lot of money. $400,000! Yours only cost you $100,000.

BOB   But I'm the older brother. I'm twenty-five and you're only eighteen.

DANIEL   Who cares about age? My Lambo is faster than your '57 BelAir. It can reach 195 miles per hour in five seconds flat.

BOB   But I built my '57 BelAir from scrap. I know
what's in it.

DANIEL   So, I got a V12. 1,234 horsepower. Ever heard
of that?

BOB   Well, if we enter my '57 BelAir this year, we
can re-enter your Lambo next year.

DANIEL   No, my Lambo should be entered every year. It's
the better car. It has a stronger engine, more horsepower, way
faster, it cost more and it is newer.

BOB   Newer isn't always better. The BelAir is a
classic. Plus, mine has four-wheel hydraulics. So, if we enter
the BelAir this year we can win the hydro contest and the best
car award.

DANIEL   Alright, we can enter your '57 BelAir. But we
better win both awards. And I get 75 percent of the winning
money.

BOB   No way! We split it fifty-fifty.

DANIEL   Fine! But we enter my Lambo next year!

        (DANIEL walks off, clearly angry, having lost the
argument.)

BOB   (Shouts) Yes!

        (BOB does a victory dance as soon as DANIEL leaves.
After that BOB gets up and exits the stage and the curtains
close.)

Felemon Helemelekhot

"THE BROKEN ARM"

(<u>JOHNSON</u> and <u>TONY</u> are playing basketball.)

<u>JOHNSON</u>   You're not good enough, Tony. If you quit now, you'll still be popular.

<u>TONY</u>   (angrily) You know what? It's none of your business if I'm not good enough. What's it to you? We've been friends ever since we were kids and you've changed a lot, Johnson. Now you're trying to make me quit basketball. What's up with that?

<u>JOHNSON</u>   You remember when we were little?

<u>TONY</u>   What are you talking about? Of course I remember! We have so many good memories!

<u>JOHNSON</u>   Try to remember very well, and think about that thing you did to me.

(<u>JAKE</u> walks onto the basketball court, ready to play.)

<u>JAKE</u>   What's up, guys? I've had a long day. Ready to play twenty-one?

<u>TONY</u>   (confused) We got a problem here. Johnson's trippin'. He's talking about the past, and asking me to quit basketball, and I just don't know what's up.

<u>JOHNSON</u>   I just still feel angry for what you did to me.

<u>JAKE</u>   What? What are you talking about?

<u>JOHNSON</u>   Don't you guys remember when you broke my arm?

JAKE   We were kids. That was an accident.

TONY   Forgive me for what I did to you! I had no idea you were thinking about that. We were just kids. And yeah, you were in the hospital for four days, but I didn't mean to hurt you!

JOHNSON   Some people, when they get hurt by others, they forget. But I can't forget it.

TONY   Just forget about it, Johnson. We have a long history together. We're young. We can do better than this. I value your friendship.

JAKE   All right, guys. Don't go getting soft on me. Let's play twenty-one!

Mustafa Ahmed

"CHOOSING ONE BALL!"

(Brothers <u>AHMED</u> and <u>KISSAM</u> are in a department store with their father <u>HASSAN</u>.)

<u>AHMED</u>   Dad, can I have a basketball?

<u>KISSAM</u>   Oh, oh, oh! Can I have a soccer ball?

<u>HASSAN</u>   Well, I only have money for one ball. You both will have to choose who gets the ball. I'm going to leave you now, because I want you to decide for yourselves. When I return in ten minutes, I want you two to have made a decision.

(<u>HASSAN</u> leaves the sports department.)

<u>AHMED</u>   I want a basketball! I don't like soccer.

<u>KISSAM</u>   Well, I don't like basketball. I want a soccer ball! Okay, okay, I have an idea. Whoever reaches the ball section first and finds the ball they want is the winner.

<u>AHMED</u>   Okay, okay, okay, I get it. Now get ready, get set, go!

<u>KISSAM</u>   Cheater! Come back! I'm going to get you!

(<u>AHMED</u> and <u>KISSAM</u> both run as fast as they can. <u>KISSAM</u>, the younger brother, runs through several wrong aisles, before he finally finds the ball section. While waiting for his brother, <u>AHMED</u> finds the basketball.)

<u>AHMED</u>   Here you are. You are the best basketball in the world, and now you're mine!

(<u>KISSAM</u> arrives at the ball section.)

<u>KISSAM</u>   You always think you can win. Look at the ball.
It's so ugly! Who wants to play basketball anyway? That game is
dumb. Soccer is much better.

          (Magic smoke appears instantly. <u>KISSAM</u> and <u>AHMED</u> cough.)

<u>AHMED</u>   Uhumph. What just happened? You did something,
didn't you, Kissam?

<u>BALL</u>   Huhm, huhm. Excuse me.

<u>KISSAM</u>   Did you hear that? Who is that?

<u>BALL</u>   It's me. Don't you see me? You, young boy! You
just insulted me. You called me ugly.

<u>KISSAM</u> & <u>AHMED</u> Whoa. The basketball is talking.

<u>BALL</u>   Haven't you seen that before? I come and go as
I wish, and I am here for one reason alone. I am very sad that
you called me ugly. What's your name?

<u>KISSAM</u>   Wha,me? Uh, Kissam.

<u>AHMED</u>   What did you do, Kissam? Now you've done
it again.

<u>BALL</u>   Calm down. I just came here to tell Kissam that
he shouldn't call anyone or anything ugly. It hurts a ball's
feelings! Besides, basketballs are great. And it's so much fun
to play with me. Why don't you give it a try, Kissam? Why would
you rather choose a soccer ball?

<u>KISSAM</u>   Uh, I don't know. Just because I like it,
and I'm good at it.

<u>BALL</u>   Aha. So you want a soccer ball just because you
are good at soccer! So maybe if you practice enough you could
be good at basketball too! I mean, just try me. Dribble me a
bit, and shoot me through a hoop. It's okay. I can take it.

KISSAM   Okay, I will try. And I'm sorry I called
you ugly.

AHMED   Yes, so we get to buy a basketball. Yes, I won!

BALL   Wait a minute. No one wins me. Everyone can
play with me!

KISSAM   I like that. Okay, well we have to go now
because our father is coming.

          (AHMED grabs the BALL. It has a smile on its face.)

HASSAN   Well sons, what have you decided?

KISSAM & AHMED The basketball!

Sadaq Abdi
Alberto Encarnacion

"THE FOOTBALL GAME"

(A friendly game of football is starting in the park.)

ZACK   Hey, you guys, it's Saturday! Let's play some
football. I'm the first captain! Called it!

ISHMAEL   Damn. All right then, I'm the second captain,
but the problem is that there are only nine of us. How are we
supposed to play?

ZACK   Each side will have four people on it, and the
one who is left will sit on the side. How does that sound?

ISHMAEL   Great, I agree.

        (ALEX enters the field.)

ZACK   Hey, look who is here! Alex, do you want to play?

ALEX   Sure. You know me, I love playing football! Put
me on whichever team you want, Zack.

ISHMAEL   What are you saying, Zack? We've already picked
teams.

ZACK   I know that, but look, this time we have one
person left on each side. We can all play now!

ISHMAEL   Hm… Okay! Alex is on my team. Everybody,
let's go! It's time to play.

ZACK   Wait, what are talking about? I saw him first!
He should be on my team!

ISHMAEL   What? Hey, am I supposed to listen to everything you say?

ZACK   Remember, I'm the first captain and I, as first
captain, am allowed to have dibs on a player.

ISHMAEL   Yeah, but you have better players than I do.

ZACK   Look, Ishmael, stop wasting time! If you don't
respect the rules of first captain than the game is off. Do you
understand?

ALEX   Hold on, hold on, guys. No need to get all up
in arms. I'm here for everybody but the rules are the rules.

          (ISHMAEL looks at ZACK.)

ISHMAEL   Don't talk to me about the rules. Ever since we
were little, and we played together, you always got your way.
You always choose the best players! That's why you always win.
I'm sick of it. I'm not gonna let you do that anymore, so I
better get Alex.

Zack   We've been through a lot together. I didn't
know that you felt like that. How about this? Let's make a
deal. I'll let you win one game if you let me keep Alex.

ISHMAEL   Let me think about it.

          (ISHMAEL leaves to get a drink of water, but shortly
returns.)

ISHMAEL   I've been thinking about it, and I trust you.
So yes, if you let me win, you could keep Alex.

ZACK   That's cool. I'll let you win. Now let's play.

ALEX   Yeah, yeah. That's what I wanna hear!

Xiaoli Yu

"LET US PLAY TABLE TENNIS"

(HEE, SB and EXP are in school.)

HEE   Let's play a game!

SB   Okay, play what? Soccer? Tennis? Or something
else?

EXP   I know, let us play table tennis!

HEE   That is easy! I will win!

SB   How do you know you will win? I am good at
table tennis!

EXP   Let's see who's really good at table tennis!
I'll be the judge because you know, I'm not very good, but I
like deciding.

(In the table tennis room.)

HEE   I'm ready.

SB   Come on! I'm ready too! We're waiting for you,
Exp.

EXP   I am ready too. Let's begin! I will sit right
over there while you both play.

HEE   I will serve the first ball. SB, are you ready
to catch the ball?

SB   Stop talking and hit the ball. Bring it on!

(Ping, Ping, Pong, Pong.)

SB   I win the first ball! Do you know what that means? I'm making a good start.

HEE   Wait and see!

(Ping, Ping, Pong, Pong.)

EXP   Hee has eleven points, SB has eight. Hee won the first round!

SB   Hurry up! Hurry up! Let's continue playing. Hee, you may have won the first round, but I'll get better.

HEE   I'll believe it when I see it.

EXP   Start the second round!

HEE & SB   Okay!

(Ping, Ping, Pong, Pong.)

HEE   What? How did I lose the second round?

SB   For thirty years a river runs east, for thirty years a river runs west. Do you know what this means? Really, you don't know? Aren't you supposed to be an expert on proverbs? Well, I'm not going to tell you!

EXP   One-One!

(Ping, Ping, Pong, Pong.)

HEE   I lost. I lost the game! I can't believe it. I never lose a game.

EXP   It doesn't matter! It's just a game!

SB   Ahahahahahahahahahahaha!

HEE   Hmm, Hmm, wait and see!

SB   What are you talking about?

HEE   When will we play table tennis again?
I want to win!

EXP   Oh come, on. Don't be a sore loser.

        (They go outside.)

EXP   What a good memory!

SB   Yes, I must admit, it was a good day.
But someone doesn't think so.

HEE   I lost, but don't get too comfortable,
I'll return.

        (Everyone goes home wondering about what might
happen next.)

Chapter 6

Indie

James D. Walker
Anthony R. Ferrer

"THE UNEXPECTED STOP!"

        (Metro bus #358. Place: Seattle, Washington approaching
the Aurora Bridge. The bus is extremely crowded. It is raining,
windy, and dangerously slippery. The bus is twenty minutes late.)

ANGRY MAN   Stupid bus! Why is it so crowded and late!
I need to get to my doctor's appointment.

SCARED KID   Shut up, sit down, and wait.

ANGRY MAN   I want to go home. I've been a teacher for four
years, and I lost my job today. I fell down the stairs, and the
kids laughed at me.

SCARED KID   I feel sorry for you, but stop yelling.

ANGRY MAN   One of the kids tripped me and I got mad. I hit
him. He deserved it.

BUS DRIVER   Aurora Bridge!

ANGRY MAN   That's my stop! 'Scuse me. 'Scuse me.

SCARED KID   (on cell phone) Hi, John? There was this man…
I'm on the bus… I think he's crazy. Hehehehe! Well, he talked
to me and said he's a teacher. No, I think he just got off.
Yeah, let's go to your house tonight. Oh! He's still on the
bus. Okay, bye.

ANGRY MAN   Excuse me, excuse me.

        (ANGRY MAN pushes people out of the way. The bus starts
to move away.)

ANGRY MAN   Wait! Stop! That's my stop!

BUS DRIVER   I can't stop now. I'm twenty minutes late! You
can get off at the next stop. I'm sorry. I'm under pressure!
It's rainy, the bus is full, the traffic is harsh. Stay back
and calm down!

ANGRY MAN   *!&! Stop the bus now or I'll use my knife! Let
me off now! I've got to see my doctor! I need my meds! I lost
my job! I'm hurt! Now let me off this bus!

BUS DRIVER   What?! What, you crazy psychopath? What are you
saying? I can't hear you. Just sit down and wait!

        (He brakes hard to avoid a car.)

SCARED KID   Look out, he has a knife!

        (SCARED KID takes out his cell phone and calls his mom.)

SCARED KID   Mom!! We're on the Aurora Bridge and I'm so
scared! There's a crazy psychopath on the bus and I think we're
going to crash. HELP ME!!!!! Okay, I am holding onto a pole. I
love you, Mom!

ANGRY MAN   Let me out of this bus now!

        (The bus hits a bump, he falls, hits a woman on her leg
with his pocket knife.)

SCARED KID   He stabbed her!! Somebody help her! She's
bleeding!

        (Everyone screams.)

ANGRY MAN   You see what happened? Now will you let me out?
It wasn't my fault!

BUS DRIVER   (shaking) We're going to crash!!!!!!

        (More screaming.)

<u>BUS DRIVER</u>   Everyone brace yourself!!! We're going over!!!

<u>ANGRY MAN</u>   I'm sorry for everything I've done! I didn't mean for this to happen!

<u>SCARED KID</u>   MOM!

Morgan Thompson

"BOB'S BAD DAY"

(BOB's house. The present. It's morning.)

BOB   Time to get up and go to the park.

(BOB walks downstairs to the kitchen and gets out a box of cereal.)

BOB   Okay! Done with breakfast. Time to go to the park!

(BOB walks to the park.)

BOB   Now that I'm at the park, it's time to hang out and play!

(BOB sees a POLICE OFFICER walking towards him.)

POLICE OFFICER Put your hands behind your back! You're going to court.

(POLICE OFFICER takes BOB to his police car. BOB is taken to court.)

JUDGE   This is case number 2,256. Let's begin! Officer, you may talk.

POLICE OFFICER Thank you, your honor. I would like to call Bob to the stand. Bob, have you ever taken drugs?

BOB   No.

POLICE OFFICER Have you ever driven drunk?

BOB   Yes, once. I was at a party and there was
lemonade that happened to have some alcohol. I didn't know it
had alcohol in it, so I drank ten glasses of it. Then I left
the party. Once I started driving, I started feeling dizzy.
Then I threw up.

POLICE OFFICER   Have you owned a gun?

BOB   No.

POLICE OFFICER   Have you been married?

BOB   Yes, once. But only for three months. Then she
dumped me.

POLICE OFFICER   Have you seen a dead person?

BOB   Yes.

POLICE OFFICER   Who?

BOB   My grandma. We were walking in the park, and
then suddenly she fell down dead!

POLICE OFFICER   Do you smoke?

BOB   Yes.

POLICE OFFICER   How old are you?

BOB   30.

JUDGE   Bob, it's your turn to speak.

BOB   Thank you, your honor. I would like to call
Police Officer to the stand.

          (POLICE OFFICER takes the stand.)

BOB   How old are you?

POLICE OFFICER   34.

BOB   How long have you been a police officer?

POLICE OFFICER   10 years.

BOB   Have you taken drugs?

POLICE OFFICER   No.

BOB   Have you ever driven drunk?

POLICE OFFICER   No.

BOB   Are you married?

POLICE OFFICER   Yes.

BOB   Do you smoke?

POLICE OFFICER   Yes.

JUDGE   Bob, you are an idiot.

BOB   Shut up, your honor.

JUDGE   I sentence you to the rest of your life
in prison.

Tammy Yu
Hussein Mohamed

"A BIT TOO HARSH"

(<u>TYLOR</u> and <u>ALYSSA</u> meet in class.)

(RRRIINNNNGGGG!!)

TYLOR   Hey, Babe!

ALYSSA   Hey!

          (She pecks him on the lips, then sits down and turns
around to face him.)

                    Did you hear we have a sub today? I heard he's
a total dork! This should be fun.

          (students talking)

TYLOR   Yeah!

          (He throws football up and down. <u>MR. DANG</u> walks into
the class.)

MR. DANG   Hush! Hush! Hush! Class has started!

          (He drops a sandwich.)

                    Oops!

          (He bends down to pick it up.)

ALYSSA   (rolls eyes) Well, that's kind of obvious!

          (students chuckle)

MR. DANG   Good morning Renton High School! So, let's begin!

       (He writes on the whiteboard.)

          My name is Mr. Dang. Mr. D-A-N-G. I will be
your Spanish substitute for today.

TYLOR   Daannggg!

MR. DANG   Let's take attendance. Everyone's here? Yes?
Okay. Let me call the attendance office.

       (He picks up the phone, then slams it down.)

          Ugh!! How do you work this thing?!

ALYSSA   Are you SERIOUSLY that dumb?!

       (She stands up and fixes her hair, then walks over and
grabs the phone, dials the number and talks on the phone.)

          Hey, Ms. Jones, this is Alyssa Tran... Hi, yes,
I'm calling for attendance... Yes... Mhm, everyone's here... Ahuh,
thank you!

       (She hangs up the phone, and turns around to look at
MR. DANG.)

          THAT'S how you work a phone, moron!

       (She walks back to desk and sits down.)

TYLOR   Ha ha!

       (Students laugh. TYLOR spits a spitball at MR. DANG.
MR. DANG grunts and adjusts his glasses.)

MR. DANG   WHO THREW THAT?!

       (students laugh)

MR. DANG   Whatever...

(He walks over to the desk and attempts to sit down, but falls.)

                    Ah! Who did this?!

ALYSSA   (to <u>TYLOR</u>.) Oh my gosh! You're so mean! Ha ha!

          (Turns to face <u>MR. DANG</u>.)

                    Maybe you're just so fat! You broke the chair!
          Now you owe the school a new chair! Loser!

          (scoffs)

MR. DANG   Mind your own business, Ms. Tran.

                    (gazes off) Unicorns are so pretty.

TYLOR   Are you an idiot or something? Wow… "Pretty."
Say "I-P-pretty colors."

MR. DANG   What? No I'm not an idiot! Uhh…

          (hesitates)

                    I-P-pretty colors…?

ALYSSA   (scoffs) LOOOOOOOSERRRR! Dork! Can you GET any
stupider?!

          (students laugh)

MR. DANG   D-D-D-D-Do you want detention?!

TYLOR   (sarcastic, mocking) Ooooh! I'm SO afraid! NOT!

MR. DANG   Let's start our lesson today then. I will hand
these out. Please turn to page three.

          (He passes books out.)

ALYSSA   Eww! Dora the Explorer?! Do we LOOK like
preschoolers?! EWW!

MR. DANG   (singing) I'm the map, I'm the map, I'm the
map, (enthusiastically) I'M THE MAP!

TYLOR   STUPID!

ALYSSA   (mocking) You're such a moron...

MR. DANG   E-E-E-Excuse me?

        (He drops his pencil.)

TYLOR   Your mother!

        (students laugh)

MR. DANG   Okay, back to the book.

        (He bends down to pick up his pencil.)

                Swiper, no swiping! Say it with me!

TYLOR   You're STUPID, man!

        (MR. DANG walks to his desk, sits down, and pulls his
hair back in frustration, then gets up.)

MR. DANG   Excuse me class, I am going to go make copies
for the quiz.

        (He walks out the door.)

        (students groan)

ALYSSA   (whispers something to TYLOR)

TYLOR   Okay! Let's start setting up! Everyone set up!

ALYSSA   (points) Get those buckets of paint! Grab the
chair and put the paint on the edge of the door! HURRY!

TYLOR   (holds his hands out) STOP! Alyssa, weren't we supposed to use those paint buckets for the Spanish mural?

ALYSSA   Whatever! Who cares!

TYLOR   Get moving! He'll come back any minute!

        (One minute later MR. DANG opens the door. Buckets of paint fall over his head.)

MR. DANG   AHHH!! AHHH!! I've HAD it! You guys are the most OBNOXIOUS, (puts fingers up) STUPID and cruelest kids on EARTH!! Good day!

        (Walks. Stops.)

                 I said, GOOD DAY!

        (MR. DANG slams the door, then comes back in and grabs his briefcase.)

TYLOR   Score!

        (high fives)

ALYSSA   Awesome!

        (high fives)

TYLOR   So what are we going to do about the consequences?

ALYSSA   I don't know. Just pretend he accidentally tripped on the paint. We're probably going to get detention. I'll just have to lie…

        (Evil glare. The phone rings. ALYSSA walks over and picks it up.)

ALYSSA   (innocently) Hello?

                 (worried) Yes. Well, he came back from the copy

room, and tripped over the buckets of paint we were supposed to use… Yes… He fell unconscious and he forgot EVERYTHING! Yes… okay. Bye bye.

TYLOR   What'd they say?

ALYSSA   Totally fell for it!

         (class cheers)

         (Thirty minutes later…)

ALYSSA   (worried) Tylor

TYLOR   (confused) Yes, hon?

ALYSSA   I kind of feel bad for what we did to him.

TYLOR   Yeah…

ALYSSA   Meet me at the front during lunch.

         (Bell rings.)

         (One hour later…)

TYLOR   Okay… I'm here.

         (He sits down next to ALYSSA.)

ALYSSA   I heard where Mr. Dang lives.

TYLOR   Ahuh…

ALYSSA   Let's go pay him a visit and apologize.

         (She gets up and starts walking.)

TYLOR   What if I don't want to go?!

ALYSSA   C'mon!

TYLOR   We were just messing with him!

ALYSSA   It was still really mean. We went a bit too far this time. Let's go!

TYLOR   (sighs)

          (Ten minutes later they arrive at MR. DANG's house. ALYSSA rings the doorbell.)

MR. DANG   (angrily) No... not you two again...

          (He attempts to shut the door.)

ALYSSA   Wait!

          (She stops the door.)

          Look... we just wanted to say sorry. I admit we were a bit too harsh.

MR. DANG   ... It's okay.

TYLOR   Yeah... I'm sorry too.

MR. DANG   It's alright.

ALYSSA   Well... We have to go now. Bye.

          (ALYSSA and TYLOR walk off as MR. DANG closes the door.)

ALYSSA   I feel like the whole world is off my shoulders now.

          (TYLOR grabs ALYSSA's hand and holds it.)

TYLOR   Let's get back to lunch.

Noah Sather
Will Fuller

"GREY AND ME"

NOTE FROM THE PLAYWRIGHTS: The character of ME should be played by two or more people.

    (GREY is walking down the sidewalk. ME steps out of the alley and grabs GREY'S sleeve.)

GREY   What are you doing?!

ME   Have you heard about the way?

GREY   Leave me be!

    (GREY starts to walk away but is held back by ME.)

ME   I see you know no meaning to your visions.

GREY   How do you know about my visions?

ME   I am one with everything, for I have accepted the truth, GREY BUTWIN.

GREY   Wait, how do you know my name? Who are you?

ME   I am Me, I am only Me, and I will never be different.

GREY   But what is your name?

ME   Did I not just tell you my name is Me? Here, have a cardboard hat. I think your son would like it as a present.

    (GREY snatches hat from ME and walks off stage in a huff.)

    (<u>GREY</u> walks into a toy store, looks around and picks something up. He looks out the window and sees <u>ME</u> staring at him.)

GREY   Great.

    (<u>GREY</u> looks away from <u>ME</u> and back again, but <u>ME</u> is gone. <u>GREY</u> looks at the toy box. The box title reads: What was wrong with the paper hat? <u>GREY</u>'s eyes go buggy. He drops the toy and rushes out of the store.)

    (<u>GREY</u> goes to a <u>PSYCHIATRIST</u> to talk about seeing <u>ME</u>.)

GREY   I keep seeing him everywhere I go.

PSYCHIATRIST   Don't worry, Grey, it is all in your head. Here is a prescription. Pay the receptionist on your way out! Next!

    (<u>GREY</u> walks out of the office into the lobby.)

    Mr. Me, I am ready for you.

    (A man stands up. It is <u>ME</u>. <u>GREY</u> leaves the room.)

    (<u>GREY</u> is walking down the sidewalk. He sees <u>ME</u> in an alley and starts to hurry toward the street corner. He sees <u>ME</u> around the corner.)

GREY   GAH! Leave me alone!

    (<u>GREY</u> pivots, runs across street away from <u>ME</u>, offstage. <u>ME</u> shakes head. <u>GREY</u> runs back in, slows down, and stops. He hears a noise behind him, whips around, and just sees a bird. He sighs and wipes his brow. He turns around again and sees <u>ME</u> standing in front of him.)

GREY   YAH! What do you want from me?

ME   I told you the truth… you scoffed. I gave you a gift… you stowed it away. I gave you a chance… you ran. Now it is time for you to be cleansed!

(<u>ME</u> raises knife. <u>GREY</u> screams. <u>ME</u> makes a stabbing motion, but right before the knife touches him, <u>GREY</u> wakes up in bed.)

<u>GREY</u>   What a strange dream!

(<u>GREY</u> reaches into his pocket and looks surprised. He pulls out a cardboard hat, examines it, and sees something inside. He reads the words written inside the hat: "I told you so.")

Sophie Johnson
Anna Wood
Vi Nguyen

Sushi Madness

(Three men named <u>PANCAKE</u>, <u>BACON</u> and <u>TURNIP</u> are near a wooden ship in a bay near their wooden boathouse. On the dock where their ship is moored <u>PANCAKE</u> walks over to the ship and climbs on.)

<u>PANCAKE</u>   Bacon, look! A ship!

(He points to the ship.)

<u>TURNIP</u>   That's our ship, Pancake!

(<u>PANCAKE</u> looks confused. <u>BACON</u> walks into the kitchen and finds hot pancakes ready.)

<u>BACON</u>   Look guys, pancakes! And they're already made! Let's eat them.

(<u>TURNIP</u> and <u>PANCAKE</u> run over.)

<u>TURNIP</u> & <u>PANCAKE</u>   Yum yum!!

(<u>BACON</u> closes his eyes and smells the sweet aroma of the pancakes. <u>TURNIP</u> grabs a hot steaming pancake and takes a bite.)

<u>TURNIP</u>   That's one good pancake!

(He gulps down the rest of the pancake. <u>TURNIP</u> reaches down to grab another pancake. <u>PANCAKE</u> slaps <u>TURNIP</u>'s hand.)

<u>TURNIP</u>   What the…?

PANCAKE   Not everybody got one, gosh tubby turnip.

TURNIP   WELL!!!

          (He recoils his hand.)

BACON   Can I have one now?

          (He shows PANCAKE his puppy dog face.)

PANCAKE   Yeah, I guess so.

          (BACON grabs PANCAKE's arm and bites down hard.)

PANCAKE   Owie!!! That hurt!

          (He rubs his bloody arm.)

BACON   No, not the sweet aroma? I imagine it's more
fleshy...

          (He pauses, chews a bit longer.)

BACON   It doesn't have syrup, that's it!

PANCAKE   Get off me, Bacon Strip!!!

          (BACON lets go of PANCAKE's arm.)

TURNIP   (chanting) Fight! Fight! Fight!

BACON   Who ya' callin' Bacon Strip? You... you buttery
piece of pancake!

          (TURNIP stops chanting.)

TURNIP   Yeah, who are you calling strip?

BACON   You're not the strip, gosh tubby turnip!

TURNIP   Yeah, but I don't like buttery pancakes... I
like syrupy ones.

PANCAKE   Hey! watch it, bub!

          (TURNIP sticks his tongue out at PANCAKE.)

PANCAKE   Hey! What was that for? Meanie!

BACON   Shut up, you stupid limp sausage!

PANCAKE   That wasn't very nice.

TURNIP   Ah, shut...

BACON   Turnip, stay out of this!

          (TURNIP stares at BACON. TURNIP starts to open
his mouth.)

BACON   (pointing to the water) Look, a fish!!!

TURNIP   It's a plump trout!!

          (TURNIP squeals frantically.)

PANCAKE   Get it, get it!!

          (BACON casts the fishing pole.)

BACON   I got it, I got it!!

          (BACON reels in the fish frantically.)

TURNIP & PANCAKE (chanting) Sushi dinner tonight!!

          (The trout flops and dangles, trying to breathe, but is
unable to.)

PANCAKE   It is squishy.

TURNIP   No, it's sushi!!!

About the Authors

We asked our student authors about themselves
and gave them this bonus question: if you had
a super power, would you want to be able to
fly, or to be invisible?

197.

SARA ABBASIAN likes being twelve because she can still get away with paying kids' prices at the amusement parks. Sara's favorite character in her play is Kim, who is wild and ignorant. Sara thinks the best part about having the power of invisibility would be getting to find out where her mom hides the Christmas presents.

Fourteen-year-old SADAQ ABDI's favorite character is Zack because he reminds Sadaq of himself. Sadaq's partner was "cool" and came up with a lot of ideas. He would rather have the power to fly because he wants to go up high in the sky "like the birds." He also likes playing sports and watching soccer or football.

AMY ACEVEDO's favorite characters in her play, Jazmin and Banana, are most interesting because they're the meanest and most mischievous. If she were invisible she might do bad things, too, but she settles for being eleven and doing fun things instead. Her favorite part of working with her partner? Sharing great ideas.

At age twelve, EVAN ADAMS appreciates that he's now old enough to make his own decisions. His play is inspired by a memory of when he and his friend made a crucial choice. Sometimes, when engaged in creative pursuits, Evan finds himself flooded with so many ideas they are difficult to comprehend. He enjoys using writing as a way to express himself.

Twelve-year-old HAMZIYE AHMED loves playing with his friends at Green Lake. His characters were inspired by his friends, and his favorite thing to do is to help people and help his mother. He would choose the power to fly.

Twelve-year-old MUSTAFA AHMED thinks it would be "really cool" to be invisible. A place inspired his play, and his favorite character is Kobe, based on the real Kobe Bryant, "because he's one of the best players in basketball." He thought it was easy to write his play, and he liked working with his writing partners.

LILI ANN ALVARADO doesn't think she would ever get tired of being invisible. In her play, however, she is visible as Nena, the character based on her. At twelve, she's already discovered the difficulties and rewards of writing a semi-autobiographical play: it is confusing, but it also can be helpful for writing what you feel.

ANDY CAO's play was inspired by a friend, but his favorite character is the one named after himself. His partner's crazy imagination spurred their writing, but Andy also wishes he could fly so he actually could go anywhere either of them could imagine. His favorite part of being thirteen? Finally being allowed to play things rated PG 13.

JUSTIN CAUBLE thinks the most enjoyable thing about being thirteen is being able to party, which is reflected in his play in the character Brock. He felt lucky to have the opportunity to write with one of his good friends. The inspiration for the story? Aliens.

JONATHAN CHAN thinks the best part of being thirteen is riding in the front seat next to the driver. His inspiration for the play was school trips to Seattle Center. The best parts of writing were sharing ideas with his partner and thinking up a name, but all the typing was hard. John loves playing with his sister and would like to be able to fly, as it would be cheaper and more energy-efficient than driving.

As a twelve-year-old, BRIER CROSS likes doing thing now that he couldn't do when he was a lot younger. One of those things? Writing epic, comedic plays. Brier's favorite character in his play is Joe because Joe is a lot like him. Independent-minded, Brier thinks invisibility is the best super power because invisible people get to go anywhere they choose.

KEVIN DANG likes everything about being thirteen, except for typing. The inspiration for his play was a memory in which he met a fake hobo who was rich, as well as a movie he watched with his dad. His favorite character is James, because he is the most complicated.

Thirteen-year-old C.J. DE LA FUENTE would like you to know that he plays basketball every day, and playing basketball inspired his play. His favorite character in the play is Jamal because he's good at playing basketball. While C.J. didn't like changing some words in the play, he did like writing about basketball. He would choose the power to fly because then he could go anywhere.

Twelve-year-old JONATHAN DEL CID was inspired to write his play by all the rich people who are losing all their money. Jonathan thinks it's important for people to admit their mistakes. His favorite character in his play is James, because eventually James realizes what he's done.

RYAN DZULKARNAEN's writing was inspired by several movies he's seen recently. His favorite part of the writing process is brainstorming because of all the crazy ideas that came up, and he really appreciated how his partner got serious at the end and helped finish a great play. While he likes being twelve and staying up late, he would love to be able to fly home to Indonesia, which he misses.

ELIJAH EDWARDS, twelve, likes staying out late and finishing writing plays! His play was inspired by Zoë, but his favorite character is Duran, because he dies.

"I always play football with my friends," says thirteen-year-old ALBERTO ENCARNACION. "So that's what inspired my play." His favorite character was Alex because he's good at football. His favorite part of the project was writing down the problem in the play and his not so favorite moment was typing it. Alberto also liked his writing partner's great ideas.

The first day of middle school: this is what GABRIEL ESTRELLA likes best about being twelve. Gabriel was a little scared that he wouldn't finish writing the play, and his favorite moment was finishing. His favorite character is Tony, and he was inspired to write the play by the memory of having bullied someone before. What did he like about working with his writing partner? "We have good ideas."

At twelve, ANTHONY R. FERRER is glad to be in his teens. Angry Man is his favorite character in the play, especially in his yelling scene at the beginning. Anthony is grateful to his intrepid co-writer for doing the typing. If he could, he would like to be able to fly, because it would be quicker than other forms of transportation.

HELEN FESSAHAIE is excited to be twelve, because it means she gets to go see her sister. She was inspired to write her play by Miss Alex and by her writing partners, who helped Helen find new words. A roving spirit, Helen would like to be able to fly so that she could travel from country to country.

Fourteen-year-old WILL FULLER is multi-talented. Not only does he write first-rate plays, he also snowboards. With a love for the big screen, Will found inspiration for his play in a movie, and enjoyed acting out his finished work. Will appreciated creating this work with his fellow playwright—a creative soul. Will considers flight the superior super power because to fly would be boss.

Thirteen-year-old MARIA GARCIA found her inspiration in her old friend Brenda and her brother. Her favorite character is Jazmin, and she has a lot of praise for her writing partners. "I really liked my partners because they made the play funny and real and made me and others laugh." Maria would fly so she could visit her family.

Having a lot of freedom is the best part of life at thirteen, says SKIAH GARDE GARCIA. Skiah describes himself as original, and finds inspiration for his work from within. Engrossed in writing his play on a ferry one day, Skiah was so startled when the horn blew, he nearly had an accident. Skiah has sympathy for his character, Mati, who is not the smartest tool in the shed.

DANIEL GONZALEZ likes being a twelve-year-old in middle school because now he gets to study interesting things in science class, like how to clean up polluted water. His play is inspired by his love for cars—specifically, Hondas. Daniel's favorite character in his play, Bob, is also a car enthusiast. One great thing about writing a play with a partner, Daniel says, is how they learn to understand each other and make choices together.

When nine-year-old DAVID GONZALEZ is not writing, he can be found riding his BMX bike or playing video games. David got inspiration for his play from the theme park, Water Rides. Like his play, Water Rides is fun, fun, fun. The best part of the playwriting process for David was coming up with the funny ending lines and mocking his character, Rich Boy. If David could be invisible, he'd do lots of things without people noticing, like opening and closing doors.

Twelve-year-old THANIA GUERRA looks to her friends when she needs inspiration. Together, she and her writing partner created lots of bright ideas, like the character Brenda, who is too cool. Thania says invisibility is the best super power because someone who's invisible can do whatever they want without anyone seeing.

TASHAWNA HANEY knows the best part of being twelve-years-old: no bills. Her play was inspired by her teacher, Mr. McEvoy, whose crazy antics resemble those of her favorite characters in her play, Kenny Biglips. Tawshawna calls her writing partner by her nickname, "Fabulosa," and appreciates her good ideas.

Seattle Center provided inspiration for ALI HASSAN's writing. His writing partner also helped him with details sometimes. Ali likes playing around with friends best about being thirteen years old. He liked the character of Eric "because he likes to sneak in." Is there anything else he'd like the world to know? "826 is one of the best groups ever."

If ELIAS MOHAMED HASSAN could fly he would fly away to Africa to see his family. What he likes best about being thirteen years old is playing with his friends. He was inspired by the movie "Shrek," and his favorite character in the play is Jeff.

The power to fly or be invisible? JUDY HE is clear about which she would pick. "I want to be invisible because like that I don't have to do something I don't want to do." Judy's favorite character is Helen because she named her, and she enjoyed working with Quan because he writes very fast. What's good about being twelve is that she's older than before.

Thirteen-year-old FELEMON HELE-MELEKHOT would like you to know that he is a "really fun boy." His imagination inspired the play, and his favorite character is Tony. He likes that the characters in the play solve their problem.

ABDULWUHAB HILOWLE thinks it's "cool" being thirteen years old, and he can't wait to get older. His own imagination inspired his writing, and he had fun writing without a partner. His favorite character is Anders. If Abdowuhab could fly or be invisible, he would choose flying for the fresh air and because he always wanted to touch the sky.

YA XIN HUANG is twelve years old, and found inspiration for her play in a memory. She is good at math. She enjoys writing collaboratively and appreciated her writing partner's spelling help. Ya Xin would like to be able to fly. Then, it wouldn't matter if she didn't have a car because she would just fly to the store.

ARIANNA HUERTAS celebrated her thirteenth birthday on Thanksgiving. She was inspired to write her play by her brother Derek, who sacrificed his dream of joining the Army so his family wouldn't worry about him. Arianna likes humorous geeks, such as the character Evan in her play. Arianna makes her friends laugh so hard they've been known to blow snot rockets of laughter in her presence.

"I like writing and I want to be an author," declares SAID IBRAHIM, who enjoys being twelve years old because he can do things other kids can't, like see scary movies. Mr. Ben is his favorite character because he takes the kids in the play to the NCAA. Said valued his writing partner C.J.'s good ideas. Said would choose the ability to fly because then he could avoid traffic jams.

At age eleven, BRANDON IRITANI notices that now he has more privileges. He is eager for the day when his privileges will include driving. Brandon's love for cars inspired his play. He appreciated his writing partner's equal enthusiasm for all things automotive. Together, they used their expertise to include lots of realistic vehicular details. What would Brandon do if he could be invisible for a day? Play tons of tricks on his brother.

SORA ISHIWATA likes feeling mature at twelve, but would like it if feeling mature came with the gift of flight. Her writing partner and her favorite character are both funny, which makes them fun to cooperate with and write about. She wishes that the aliens who inspired the play also could have taken care of the typing.

JORDYN JARVIS craves variety in her life. She appreciates that now, as a twelve-year-old, she gets to change classes throughout the school day. Jordyn likes the potential she feels at the start of projects, and thus enjoyed writing the first draft of her play. She appreciated working with her writing partner, who has many skills. Among them, she's a really fast typist.

At twelve, VERONICA JOHANSON enjoys being wild, and not caring what people think of her yet. Adventurous and strong—these are two character attributes she admires. Veronica was inspired to write by her cousin Anthony, who lives in Virginia and is almost in college. Veronica enjoyed working on her play with her friend and writing partner, Ari, who made her laugh.

SOPHIE JOHNSON is twelve years old and has a dreamy imagination. Thinking about being realistic is her least favorite part about playwriting. Laughing with her collaborators is her favorite. Sophie loves working with her writing partners because they are her best friends in the whole world. Got that, punk? She emphasizes.

The best thing about being eleven years old is that "you can go to the store by yourself," says UM KALSOOM. She liked spending time with her friends while writing the story, and liked that her writing partners helped with parts of the story. Her favorite characters are Min and Johana "because they have lots of details."

BICIOK KIIR would pick the power to fly because then he wouldn't have to walk anymore. All of his Hispanic friends inspired his play, and his favorite character is Juan because he comes up with the idea to jump the border. He loved creating the idea for the play. What is the best thing about being thirteen years old? Having authority over little kids.

WYATT LEASE is twelve years old. He looks to a variety of sources for ideas in his writing. His muses for this play? His writing partner and a squirrel. He enjoyed the former because he was fun to hang out with. The squirrel may or may not have been fun as well.

Teachers inspire twelve-year-old KATY LEI when she writes. With her finely tuned ear for speech, Katy's forte is capturing realistic dialogue. Katy likes creating characters that develop and change. Her favorite character in her play is Jake, who learns an important lesson from his brother.

"I can take the Metro bus by myself." This is what QUAN LOU likes best about being twelve years old. His favorite character in the play is Lauren because she is a "nice girl," and he enjoyed working with his writing partners. Sometimes writing the play gave Quan a headache, but he also got a lot of ideas for it during homeroom.

MANUEL LOYA likes the freedom of being twelve, though it would be increased by invisibility. In his play, which was inspired by the good and bad things in life, his favorite character is Slappy because he resorts to crazy stuff to distract Fred. He also enjoyed working with his smart, food-loving writing partner.

FATUMA MAHMUD would like you to know that she didn't speak English until she was ten years old. Now that she is twelve, she likes having her own bedroom. Fatuma liked that she and her writing partner helped each other. She would choose both being able to fly and being invisible, and she would love to "see the birds flying with you."

LINA MAKI is twelve and has always wanted to fly. She enjoyed the process of working with her partner because Mitzy approached the play with an open mind and they found lots to laugh about as they wrote. Despite learning how difficult revision can be, Lina still likes the characters Nataly and Shelby because they are so different but like the same person. Her favorite part of being twelve? Staying up with friends all night to do crazy stuff!

What does ELIEZER MARQUEZ GERONIMO think is best about being eleven years old? "You get stronger." He would like to see how it feels to fly around like a bird, so he would choose the power of flight. His favorite character in the play was Jeff "because he is the strong one." He liked that his writing partner told jokes.

KRISNA MANDUJANO MAZARIEGOS would like to be invisible so her mom wouldn't wake her up for school. Her favorite part of being eleven, so far, is dressing up for the Halloween party at the skating rink. The group she worked with on this play was incredibly helpful, except when they accidentally collided during a rehearsal. Her favorite character in the play? Johana, because she's funny.

Why would ADAM CHRISTOPHER MASCHERI like the power to fly? "It would save time [and] gas" and there would be "no more traffic." What he likes best about being twelve is having more freedom. His favorite character in the play is Slappy, and he liked his writing partner because he skateboards, he's smart, and he's cool.

MARIA MCCARTHY thinks the best part about being twelve is going to Catharine Blaine Middle School. Maria likes peaceful people, like the character Ruby in her play, who solves conflicts. If Maria could choose a super power, she'd pick flight so she could fly away from people who bother her. Maria would definitely not fly away from her two beloved cats Honey and Smokey.

VADIM MERENOVSKIY liked working with his smart partner, who helped him expand the idea of the play. Manta is his favorite character, because he is entertaining. At twelve, Vadim wishes he could fly invisibly because if you're going to wish, you might as well wish big.

When searching for inspiration for his play, thirteen-year-old HUSSEIN MOHAMED turned to a memory of a substitute teacher. Hussein thinks life as a teenager is all right, but sometimes he hates it. He gravitates to the technological aspects of play writing, and enjoyed typing his work on the computer. Hussein appreciates working in teams, and describes his writing partner as a nice person.

BRENDA MORALES likes being twelve because it means she's not that old, but still older, and cooler, than she was in sixth grade. Her favorite character in her play is Lisseth, who is perhaps one of the most interesting people ever. She likes writing dramatic fight scenes, but dislikes when writing takes too long.

JAZMIN MORENO is twelve and is grateful that, with the exception of homework, she doesn't have too many obligations at this point in her life. Her favorite character in her play is Michael, who is really smart for an eight-year-old boy. A classic dramatist, Jazmin made sure revenge was a central theme to her play. She relied on her writing partner for comic relief and the funny stuff.

At age ten, ELI MROZEK has already experienced some disappointments—he got the idea for his play from a let down by some friends. But Eli admires people who are resilient and self-confident in the face of challenges, like Steven, the main character in Eli's play, who is "empowered." If Eli could choose a super power, he'd go with invisibility. Then, if under attack, he could magically morph into a phantom and become invincible.

KHANH TRINH NGUYEN likes going to scary movies in theaters, but it's not as much fun when his sister scares him. The best thing about being twelve is reading comic books. In his play, which was inspired by a place, his favorite character is Yoh, because he is lazy.

Twelve-year-old MELINA NGUYEN-REYES never knows when inspiration for her writing will strike. Her ideas just pop up. Melina likes people who follow through. Her favorite character in her play, Angela, is someone who can really stick with a plan. Given her choice, Melina would pick the power of flight over invisibility. Why? "Don't question me," Melina says.

MY LINH NGUYEN is twelve and thinks a lot about family. Her father inspires her to write, and shows her how to be nice and kind. My Linh has a three-year-old brother, which means she's had to get used to sharing her parents' attention. One of the primary characters in My Linh's play, Maya, is close to her family, too. My Linh likes Maya because Maya turns down a friend's advice to run away from home.

THAO-NGUYEN NGUYEN thinks it's "pretty fun" being thirteen years old. Her play was inspired by a place she saw in a movie, and her favorite character is Karin because she's a fun tomboy. Thao-Nguyen worked with Quan and Judy, who gave her a lot of ideas and helped her. If she could have the power to fly or be invisible, she'd pick both.

To twelve-year-old VI NGUYEN, bacon isn't just a breakfast food. It's also the name of her favorite character in her play. Her writing is inspired by her friends, who are usually nice but sometimes mean. That's okay, though, because friendship, with all its ups and downs, is important. If Vi could become invisible, she'd use her power to play tricks on people.

Eleven-year-old CHLOË NOONAN was inspired to write her play by a messy incident involving a mug of hot cocoa and gravity. Chloë's main character, Alex, is remarkable because she's aggressive and funny, even though she forgets what day of the week it is. Chloë enjoyed creating the character Alex with her two friendly, cooperative writing partners. If Chloë could fly, she would conceal herself in the clouds, and win every game of hide and seek.

In writing this play, SOPHIA PADILLA was inspired by a book she read recently. She really enjoyed acting out the play as she worked on it, especially the evil character Cloe. Her favorite thing about being twelve is new independence, but it would also be nice to be able to fly.

For TIFFANY PHAM, being thirteen years old means starting to prepare for the future, to think about who she wants to be and how. She was inspired by questions about what love means. "Love can hurt people and also help people." Her favorite memory of the project is how much she learned about writing a story, and she has plans to write a new story and post it to her blog.

TARA PHENIX-TOUSLEE, twelve, would like the ability to fly because of the fame it would bring. In her play, which was inspired by a person and a memory, her favorite part is when the characters get rescued and her favorite character is Adrian, who is in all the funny parts. Her helpful writing partner typed up all five pages, but Tara inserted funny comments to keep her laughing throughout.

ANTHONY QUINTO-TILA liked working with his partner, whose sense of humor made a big difference in their play. He set the play in the Galapagos because he likes penguins (despite the lack of penguins in the play). Being twelve, he finds, means people rely on you and you can begin to look forward to driving. His favorite character? Antwon, because he is wild, funny, and has a lot of imagination.

Twelve-year-old ESTEFANY SAHAGUN already has destinations in mind should she ever gain the power to fly: Mexico, Fuji, the Bahamas, or Hawaii. In the meantime, her writing was inspired by television shows, and she valued her writing partner's great ideas and funny language. Her favorite character was Paco "because he's nice, cute, strong."

In writing this play, twelve-year-old ANGEL SANDOVAL was inspired by the video game Resident Evil. He likes the character of Dustin the most because he has a big role and "shoots more zombies." If Angel could pick between the power to fly and the power to be invisible, he would choose flying, "so when I miss the bus I could fly to school."

NOAH SATHER's favorite part of being fourteen is that his brain is getting more complex, and he can think about more complicated issues. The desire to channel the strange thoughts in his brain into a character was a source of inspiration for Noah's work. His

favorite character is his play is aptly named "Me." Like Noah, Me has some strange ego issues that leak out once in a while.

Nine-year-old JASMINE SUN writes about peacemakers. Her favorite character in her play is Ruby, who tries to resolve her friends' conflict by showing them an alternative to fighting. Jasmine overflows with ideas, and loves the process of getting all her thoughts out in an initial draft. She looks to her writing partner, a good friend, for tips on revising plays and life.

Nine-year-old MORGAN THOMPSON likes the later bedtime that comes with his advancing maturity. Now, he has more time to write and create intriguing characters such as Bob, a central figure in his play. If Morgan could choose a super power, he'd pick flight. Then, he'd impress all his bus-riding friends by flying to school.

MITZY TORRES BROWN enjoyed rehearsing with her partner, Lina. She likes being thirteen because of all the sneaky things you can do, but thinks it would be even better if she were invisible—then, if she did something bad, she could just disappear. Her writing was inspired by someone she knew named Denzel, but her favorite character is Shelby.

JONATHAN TRAN says one perk of being a twelve-year-old is you can't go to prison. Also, you get to play lots of games. Jonathan was inspired to write his play by an unspecified "Halloween thing." Jonathan thinks his writing partner is great because he plays football. If he had his choice of super powers, Jonathan would pick invisibility because, then, he could escape with ease.

RIAN TRINH is happy to be twelve, because it means being in the seventh grade. His writing partner, who helped with grammar and ideas, is also the model for his favorite character in their play. He'd like to be invisible, because it would make it much easier to do things secretly.

FABIENNE VIGIL likes being able to "do more things" now that she's thirteen years old. Her favorite character in the play was Kenny because "he's a sweet little boy." She thought her writing partner was very creative and had great ideas. Fabienne would choose to fly so she could go places faster.

"It's nice to be trusted with your surroundings," says ELIZABETH C. WEST. For her, being twelve means that people look at you in a different way, "a good different," and they trust you more. Lizy (as her friends call her) was inspired to write her play by her love of horses and her friend Susan's horse, Earl. She liked the experience of changing real people's names and events into a play and working more with dialogue. "You have to think about if someone would actually say what you're thinking."

ZOË WHITE, at twelve, is savoring her independence. Her play was inspired by her best friend, but her favorite character is Jordan because of the role he

plays in the story. She loved the brainstorming part of writing, but taking it home to finish it was harder. Inspired by her partner's humor and imagination, Zoë would like to be invisible so she could play good jokes on people.

Thirteen-year-old AUGUST WOLGAMOTT finds inspiration for her writing from her friends. The best part of writing a play? Coming up with the initial idea. The worst part? Writer's block. August thinks flight is the best superpower because flying is "hella tight."

Now that she's twelve, ANNA WOOD likes that she can fit into more clothes from her favorite stores. Anna likes upbeat people, such as the character Turnip in her play, who is funny and likes to cheer people up. If granted the power of invisibility, Anna would poke her writing partners in the head, undetected.

SHEENIE SHANNON YIP is twelve, but is often mistaken for older. Her play was inspired by a British drama exam she took in Shanghai, and by her hatred for the color yellow. Sheenie's favorite part of creating her own play was, after the initial hurdle of starting, she was flooded with so many ideas, she just kept writing and writing.

ANNA YU would like to be invisible because she doesn't want people to know her. But here are a few details anyway: Anna thinks the best thing about being twelve years old is having long hair. The character she created, Lona, is her favorite because the story about her is true. Anna has good

memories of her friend helping her
with details for the play.

Twelve-year-old TAMMY YU likes
being independent. She was
inspired to write by a very spe-
cific individual. Not wanting her
dramatic homage to be too obvious
however, Tammy says she tweaked
her caricature a little. Tammy's
favorite character from her play
is Mr. Dang because he is clumsy.
What makes Mr. Dang special? He is
the cherry on top of the sundae.

XIAOLI YU wishes he could fly,
but not that he were invisible,
because he'd like people to see
him flying. His favorite thing
about being eleven is sleeping,
but he also likes table tennis.
His play's main character was also
its inspiration.

Independent-minded JING YI ZHEN
thinks the best thing about being
twelve is that she can go out by
herself. She likes yoga, and she
values honesty. She describes
Lily, her favorite character in
her play, as truthful. Given the
choice, she would pick invisibility over the power of flight,
because then, when she feels sad,
no one could see.

PEOPLE WHO HELPED MAKE THIS BOOK

Many people from 826 Seattle have made this book possible. They tutored students, copyedited stories, designed the book, managed the tutors, oversaw book production, ordered invitations, translated invitations, wrote the grant to realize this project, made the tamales, filled the milk glasses, baked the cakes, and swept the floor for the publishing party. We think that all of these people have giant hearts and believe in the power of writing. They are (in alphabetical order):

JUSTIN ALLAN
ALEX ALLRED
NORMA ANDRADE
KIT BAKKE
JIM BECKMANN
ZACH BRITTLE
JANET BUTTENWIESER
MARTHA CLARKSTON
JACOB COVEY
ALICIA CRAVEN
ANNIE DOCZI
RORY DOUGLAS
RAMÓN ESQUIVEL
ALISON GALINSKY
ALEXANDRA HALSEY
KATHY HASHBARGER

ELIZABETH HEFFRON
TERI HEIN
JEN KOOGLER
MARGARET KULKIN
NANCY JOHNSON
LEANNE LAUX-BACHAND
TOFFER LEHNHERR
JARED LEISING
JULIA LITTLEFIELD
JAYA CONSER LAPHAM
COREY MAHONEY
DAVIDA MARION
IAN MESSERLE
JEN MOORE-ARTERBURN
EMMA PARKER
KELLY PARKER

DEVYN PEREZ
KEITH QUATRARO
CLAIRE RICCI
BARBARA ROTTER
FUMIKO SCHUAB
JENNIE SHORTRIDGE
MATT SMITH
BILL THORNESS
SANDY TRIBOTTI
GWEN WEINERT
EMILY WEST
BRAD WILKE
DOUG WOODBURY

This project would not be possible without the effort and dedication from many staff at Hamilton International Middle School and students' family members. They taught, translated, administered, managed permission slips, fixed computer problems, cleaned up, and kept our student authors working on deadline. They are (in alphabetical order):

JESELY ALVAREZ
WENDY CHAPMAN
SHEILA DE LA CRUZ
KATIE CRYAN LEARY
THUY HO

CHRIS LA ROCHE
CHRIS MCEVOY
MUSSE MOHAMED
BOON SIEW
FIKRE YOHANNES

LINDA HARVELAND
MARIA CRUZ
NHAN NGUYEN

Special thanks to the SEATTLE FOUNDATION and the ANNE V. FARRELL LEADERSHIP GRANT for funding the work of 826 Seattle at Hamilton International Middle School.

8 2 6
S E A T T L E

826 Seattle is dedicated to helping young people improve their
expository and creating writing skills through free tutoring,
mentoring, workshops, and other writing programs.

"Because in our culture the ability to express oneself
effectively opens large doors."

826 Seattle Board of Directors: